MW00977366

Starving America

by

Alfred Watterson McCann

APPLEWOOD BOOKS
Bedford, Massachusetts

Starving America

was originally published in

1913

ISBN: 978-1-4290-1203-4

Thank you for purchasing an Applewood book.
Applewood reprints America's lively classics—
books from the past that are still of interest
to the modern reader.
For a free copy of
a catalog of our
bestselling
books,
write
to us at:
Applewood Books
Box 365
Bedford, MA 01730
or visit us on the web at:
For cookbooks: foodsville.com
For our complete catalog: awb.com

Prepared for publishing by HP

STARVING AMERICA

ALFRED W. McCANN

THIS PICTURE OF THE AUTHOR'S YOUNGEST CHILD, WHO HAS NEVER BEEN SICK, IS INCLUDED BY REQUEST OF THE PUBLISHER AS THE BEST EVIDENCE OF THE SOUNDNESS OF THE VIEWS ON FEEDING CHILDREN AS SET FORTH IN THE FOLLOWING PAGES.

STARVING
AMERICA

BY

ALFRED W. McCANN

MEMBER OF VIGILANCE COMMITTEE,
THE ASSOCIATED ADVERTISING
CLUBS OF AMERICA

NEW YORK
GEORGE H. DORAN COMPANY
CLEVELAND : F. M. BARTON

Copyright, 1912,
By George H. Doran Company

PREFACE.

During his seventeenth and eighteenth years, the writer suffered a severe illness which resisted treatment for eighteen months. This experience resulted in a keen interest in the subject of food. After his recovery, brought about finally by dietetic treatment, he was thrown into daily association for two years with Professor James R. Campbell, then an instructor in chemistry at Pittsburg College. His room in the college adjoined Professor Campbell's room, and they spent much time together in the discussion of chemical theories, and their experimental proofs. He conceived a profound veneration for the mysteries of organic life, and began to look upon food as the embodiment of all the forces, which, when properly co-related and released, are responsible for the continuation of life.

As an amateur, he began to study biochemistry, and the chemistry of foods, but could find nothing authoritative on the subject. Dietitians were dividing food into four groups: Carbohydrates, proteins, fats and "ash." The division of "ash" was always exasperatingly ignored, and apparently had little if any meaning for the dietitian, and was not considered by him as significant or important.

In the meantime, the writer learned that a diet of pure carbohydrates, pure proteins and pure fat, would not support life, and the subject of "ash" grew more formidable and more fascinating. Physicians and chemists everywhere, admitted that personally they knew nothing about "ash" in relalationship to food, and did not know where to go to get such information. Years of wrestling with the word "ash" resulted in little that could be depended upon until an experiment during a very critical period in the writer's life began to throw a feeble light upon the subject.

During this period, he was earning his livelihood as an advertising man, though the study of biochemistry has been of absorbing interest to him at all times.

Then it happened that he was appointed advertising manager of a large department store, which operated a grocery department, and a new avenue of a peculiar kind of information was thus opened up to him.

During the two years of his service in this capacity, he acquired fragmentary knowledge of conditions which the outside world did not suspect.

Then another and almost bottomless fountain of information concerning modern food conditions was tapped. He became the advertising man of a large food industry, and for five years his constant daily associates were food inspectors, chemists connected with the national and state departments, food manufacturers, importers, jobbers and commission men.

For three years of this five-year period, he was employed under the roof of a modern food factory, and spent a great deal of his time in the laboratory of that factory.

All the while, light was breaking upon the subject of "ash," and the facts revealed in this book were applied to the diet of his children, with results that confound nearly all accepted notions of feeding children.

During this time, Dr. Wiley was leading a great food-reform movement. The writer began working with him and for him, and by virtue of his position was able to encourage and promote many food reforms in a purely commercial way. His motives were continually assailed, because of his commercial affiliations, and it was even said by enemies of food-reform, that he had an ax to grind, and was making money out of his position.

The writer had always a strong belief that the food-reform movement would work out its own destiny, and, in his position as advertising manager, sought by every means at his disposal, to put this belief into action, but, with a specialized knowledge of modern food conditions acquired by years of service on the inside behind the screens, and with a clear understanding of the limitations of the modern food industry, he no longer expects a great food-

reform to come through advertising as now conducted.

The advertising manager cannot state the whole truth in a food advertising campaign, for the reason that those who pay the advertising bills rightly insist that their advertisements shall center about the talking points that will sell their product, always keeping clear of trespass upon ethical ground.

The food manufacturer fears to step outside the limits of a careful conservative campaign, because he feels that a radical departure from trade customs would jeopardize his business. As a commercial institution, he declares that his chief function is not to educate the masses, and points to the fact that no profit is to be derived from such policy.

Because of these obstacles in the way of reform, the writer no longer looks to commercial publicity, or to legislation as means through which to enlighten the people. Most of the conditions described here are unknown to our legislative bodies, and it will be a long time before Congress can be educated to that point, where the distressful facts here outlined will be noted and acted upon.

The reform work must be done in the schools.

Our children must be taught the meaning of depraved foods. They must learn how those foods are processed, bleached, colored, de-natured, de-germinated, de-mineralized, chemically treated. They must be taught the relationship of such food to sickness and death. They must be taught the relationship of natural food to health and life. The true conditions, now concealed from the public, must be exposed, in order that the public may make its own choice, guarded by a complete knowledge of facts. These facts are presented here in a manner understandable to the layman for the first time, and with the addition of the Catechism of Vital Questions and Answers, this work places before the people a full and complete exposure of the evil conditions, which, unmolested, now menace the health and life of America.

Lewis B. Allyn
Westfield, Massachusetts
DEPARTMENT OF CHEMISTRY
STATE NORMAL SCHOOL

October,19
1912.

My Dear McCann:

Your book has staggered me. It is startling,
appalling. You do not know how much it disturbs me.
Its force is terrific, its logic invincible.

I do not know of any other man who would dare
wrestle with the problem as you have done. Who will have the
courage to publish this book?

Certainly from now on you will be lashed and
ridiculed and hated in many quarters and heavy pressure will
be applied to keep the truth in the darkness of controversy,
but through it all your merciless analysis will stand naked
to compel attention.

Vast upheaval will come out of your work and
I shall not be greatly surprised to see after its publication
the spirit of a great and helpful revolution at our doors.

When I told you that no book of a hundred years
would equal the constructive force of yours, I meant it.
I can conceive of nothing so tremendous, so stirring, so over-
whelming as the manner in which you have presented our greatest
national menace and its remedy.

Your sincere

Lewis B. Allyn

CONTENTS

CHAPTER I.

THE BIRTHDAY PARTY.

There was something cruel in the shrill five o'clock whistle, that released the flour-mill workers from their toil, but no man heard its tragic note. It meant only that the day's labor was finished, and the workers were glad. Had there been a prophet on the street corner, to interpret the meaning of that screaming steam for them, as they came down the factory steps, they would have laughed and gone their various ways, some into convenient saloons, others hurriedly to their homes.

One man, tall, pale, neatly dressed, clerk of the factory office, stopped a moment as the men broke line, and said to himself: "How many of these poor fellows are blessed at home with a little Helen like mine?" The very thought of the child seemed to soften the hard lines of his serious face, and unconsciously he smiled.

"I guess they all have their little birthday parties, too," he said to himself, and with a quick step, he set out for the nearest candy shop.

He had left the office promptly, and other whistles were blowing, but their shrill screams had no message for his light heart.

For a whole week, little Helen had reminded him almost every day not to forget to bring candles for the great birthday cake, about which there had been so much planning at home, and he had remembered them a dozen times that day.

Seven different kinds of candy, of seven different colors to catch the children's eyes, and seven pretty candles were purchased, and snugly tucked into the deep pockets of his overcoat.

"Life is indeed worth living," he murmured buoyantly, as he turned off the main thoroughfare into the street that led to his door.

The weather was raw and chilly, so mother did not allow the little girl to run as usual to meet her father. She caught cold easily, and each cold seemed more difficult to cure than the one before. So her face was pressed against the window, as she waited eagerly for her father's coming.

As he approached the door, he saw beside the last of the year's geraniums on the sill within, the darling face of his little one against the pane. For the first time in seven years, a convulsive shudder passed over him, as he caught sight of those white little cheeks, but it was as meaningless to him in that moment, as the shrill factory whistle to the men whom he had left a half hour before.

Helen was in his arms. He lifted her high, and holding her aloft, he noted again the white cheeks of his angel, and looked into her laughing eyes stupidly.

Something in the grim and sudden drooping of his mouth transmitted itself into the mother's heart, and she turned away from her husband's gaze, and looked over the housetops into the gathering darkness. No one may know the things she saw.

"Did you bring my candles, papa?" cried the little one as she spied his bulging pockets.

"Did I?" came the proud and laughing answer. "Well just look here," and the packages were opened.

"See the purple one? that's for our little queen, and the white one is for our little queen's heart, and the blue one is for her eyes, and the golden one is for her hair, and some day"—his voice dropped a little, "and some day, our little queen's lips will be like the red one, and her cheeks like the pink one. See, aren't they pretty, these birthday candles, with a color for every candle, and a candle for every year of our little darling's life, with this big green candle for the summer Sundays, when we will all go again with our luncheon to the green woods?"

The next day little Helen's playmates came, and the birthday party with its great frosted cake, and its lighted candles, and ice cream bricks, red, and white, and green, and brown, and the fancy candy of seven different hues made a riot of color for all. The children were transported with the rainbow goodies before them. Such chatter, and clatter, and laughter and song with little Helen crowned in a whole afternoon of childhood's glory, could not be crowded within four home walls. Some of its fullness must flow over into the busy streets, and be heard far off, even in the heart of a father busy at his work three miles away.

All the afternoon he heard, he saw, he knew, and when that shrill whistle sounded again, he had forgotten the strange pain of the night before, and was off, for at least an hour of the party was to be reserved for his arrival.

They were happy "good-night" wishes that ended that happy day, and when little Helen's mother tucked her away in her warm little bed, she, too, was happy.

The next day Helen did not feel well, and did not go to school. She had a little fever, which her mother called an "upset." The fever continued another day, and they called a doctor. He felt her pulse, looked at her tongue, and asked what she had been eating.

When told about the birthday party, he smiled, and said she had probably eaten too much. He gave her some medicine, and in a few days she apparently was well again.

The doctor did not know, that the milk of which that ice cream had been made was "loose milk." He did not know that a microscopical examination of it would have revealed 90,000,000 organisms to the cubic centimeter, which is much less than a teaspoonful. He did not know that many of those organisms were of a pathogenic character. He did not know that the ice cream was stiffened with a "bodifier" made of commercial gelatin, which the Bureau of Chemistry at Washington, has shown to contain as many as 6,000,000,000 organisms to the gram, of which there are twenty-nine in a single ounce. He did not know that among those organisms were some of the most deadly forms of bacterial life.

He did not know that those colored candies were made chiefly of glucose, sweetened with about 10% of sugar. He did not know the action of glucose, and "refined" sugars when excessively consumed. He did not know that on a glucose diet, bees and white mice are quickly killed, although it has been generally supposed that glucose is a good food for the child. He did not know that the flavors of that ice cream and candy were derived from ethers, and were purely artificial. He did not know that their colors were "certified" coal tar dyes, and so he charged Helen's illness to "overeating," but he did not place much importance upon the food itself, which she had over-eaten.

Let us sit down to-night at the dining table in one of our average homes, where there are children, and discuss this thing sensibly, frankly, fully. Let us learn why Helen caught cold so easily, and why it was difficult to cure those colds, and why she had periodical "upsets."

Let us hear the real note in that shrill mill whistle, and let us seriously face the issue as parents, teachers, or physicians. We will discover what undermined the health of that little girl, and destroyed the happiness of that little family.

Of what did their breakfast consist? Let us see. There was the usual coffee, and the usual rolls and toast, with one of the many popular breakfast foods, served with milk produced by cows fed on demineralized brewer's grain, and by-products of the cotton seed oil, and glucose industries. Is this not the breakfast of millions? you ask. Stop, for this is serious business that we are discussing. There must be no argument, until all of these cruel pages have surrendered all their cruel facts to all the flour-mill and food factory whistles of America, that their warning may be heard and understood. After that, the argument, but now the food of the child.

Breakfast foods, corn, barley, wheat and rice must "keep." They must look "nice." The spirit of little Helen is asking, "By what processes are these two requirements fulfilled?"

The pages that follow will answer, and if the answer cuts deep into hearts that have been pierced already, let the later wounds inspire atonement. We have gathered together for the sake of the child.

At noon, as the father did not come home, the mother fried the potatoes left from the last night's meal, and added a bit of bologna or cheese. Helen liked bread or biscuits with syrup for lunch. Helen's mother did not know what had been taken out of the bread and biscuits, and what had been taken out of the corn that produced the syrup. She liked strawberry jam, or some other fruit jam from the grocery store, with its 10% of fruit, and its 10% of apple juice, made from the sulphured skins and cores of the dried apple industry, with its 70% of glucose, sweetened with 10% of sugar, and held together with enough inorganic phosphoric acid to supply the jellying quality, and preserved with "one-tenth" of one percent benzoate of soda, to prevent the mass from fermenting.

Only "one-tenth of one percent" of this chemical is declared on the label. The presence of as much as four more tenths of benzoate of soda in many food products was determined by the Commissioner of Agriculture of the State of Georgia, through the report of the State Chemist, published as serial number 56, in September, 1912, in spite of the fact that only "one-tenth" was declared on the label of those products. Little Helen's doctor did not know this.

Little Helen's father and mother were not taught the chemistry of food in the schools, nor the relation-ship which refined food would some day bear to their anemic child.

But we must not go too fast. The evening meal was quite suited to the father's needs. It consisted of chops, or pot roast, or sausages, or baked beans and ham, with vegetables of the season, fresh, or vegetables of some other season, canned, and a home-made pie or pudding. It was the average American meal, and it is the average meal with which we are concerned.

During the afternoon, a confectionery store down the street received many of the pennies of the little girl. It had existence for the purpose of attracting those pennies. There are just twenty million of such pennies spent each day in the United States, by school children. Helen "feasted" between meals on colored glucose at the candy store.

She had been always of a delicate type, anemic and nervous. At different times she had been treated by the family physician for tonsilitis, acute chorea and anemia. At the age of six she underwent an operation for adenoids. In the United States at the same time, there were more than 200,-000 such operations among the children. She had taken a tonic of iron and manganese.

Remember these words, "iron and manganese."

At other times tonics of strychnia were prescribed, and on two occasions she was given bychloride mercury, and chloride arsenic.

Her teeth, like those of other millions of children were decayed. At times mother said, "I wonder if we feed Helen properly?" but Aunt Jennie always answered, "Her ills are natural to childhood, and to be expected. She will outgrow them." The neighbors told her that the less attention she paid to her child's food, the better, because people who were always worrying about food had the hardest luck. Here and there a plump child was pointed out to her, as a model of what eating "anything and everything" would produce. It was not known that the plump child's plumpness had nothing to do with muscle-tone; nothing to do with normal functioning; nothing to do with vitality or high resistance. It was not known that the plump child fed on "everything and anything," succumbed even more quickly than the thin child, but grandmothers and mothers had fed children for ages, and surely they must know a little about their business. So little Helen's mother felt that, as they said, the child would eventually outgrow her illness.

A few weeks after the birthday party, as Helen was going home from school, she was caught in a rainstorm. Her mother changed her clothes as soon as she came home and gave her a hot lemonade. That night she had a high fever and again the doctor was called.

When he came, he uttered one word, "pneumonia."

That father and mother in the year 1910, stricken into dumb and sudden darkness, in the tenderest and brightest hour of their sweetest hope, faced the same unutterable emptiness of life that a quarter of a million of other fathers and mothers in the same year faced. For in the United States, in the year 1910, 235,262 little children under ten years of age, went into the great beyond, to give testimony to the darkness of earth.

The apparent cause of Helen's death was pneumonia. The real cause was mal-nutrition, low resistance, insidious starvation.

If 235,262 children had lost their lives in an epidemic, or in a massacre, it would have aroused the nation, but if those 235,262 little children travel obscurely in one year into death, the nation neither heeds nor understands.

When the Titanic went down with 1600 souls aboard, the cities of civilization put on an inky cloak of sorrow. The multitudes of many lands stood at the edge of the sea, calling through the night in their desperation, for the waters to bring their fellows home. Less than two thousand perished, but they perished in a heap. Man's power for them had come to an end. Beaten and humbled by the senseless block, the earth was dazed, because the tragedy was strange and sudden. The slow moving, deadlier peril that walks with us in the day and sleeps by our side at night, arouses no man.

Are we insensible to this fearful loss, because our children fall quietly like the petals of autumn roses? Have we grown careless to this fearful loss, because it goes on day by day, increasing each year? Do we not care to take the trouble to learn its cause?

A Bulletin prepared in 1912 by the United States Bureau of Education states that:

400,000 children have organic disease
1,000,000 children have tuberculosis in some form
1,000,000 children have spinal curvature
1,000,000 children have defective hearing
4,000,000 children are suffering from mal-nutrition
6,000,000 children have enlarged tonsils, adenoids or other gland diseases
10,000,000 children have defective teeth
15,000,000 children need attention for physical defects which are prejudicial to health.

On January 24th, 1912, the census director at Washington issued mortality statistics for 1910, revealing for that year, 805,412 deaths in the United States. Roughly tabulated some of these are—

Infants under one year of age............ 154,375
Children from two to five years of age.... 62,946
Children from six to ten years of age...... 17,943

Total deaths of children under ten.... 235,262
Youths from ten to 19 years of age...... 31,508
Deaths between 20 and 29 years of age.... 62,957
Deaths between 30 and 39 years of age.... 68,957
Deaths between 40 and 49 years of age.... 72,935

The appalling sacrifice of infants indicates that nearly 200,000 American women entered into the shadows of motherhood unfit to bring their children into the world, or having brought them into the world, were unfit to care for them. With such a background as this, our proud parade of Paris fashions in softly folded tissues, delicate silks, and wools, ravishing creations, takes on the leer of refined debauch.

Two hundred and thirty-five thousand two hundred and sixty-two little children in the rear of that parade were denied the right to enter their "teens" and many thousands of young men and women facing life with all its possibilities went wearily into the great beyond while the heart of womanhood was brooding over the captivating styles of dress.

A study of these brutal facts should not alarm us. It should inspire hope. By ignoring the truth or by refusing to look into it because of the grim depression which accompanies the contemplation of such a holocaust, we betray our unfitness to deserve a better fate.

By facing the situation bravely and by determining to find out the cause of America's Slaughter of the Innocents we prove that in some measure at least we are worthy to account for our stewardship of the lives that have been put into our keeping.

If in the year 1912 a hostile army should visit our shores and put to death a quarter of a million of our young people, there would be weeping and wailing and gnashing of teeth. We would cry to heaven for vengeance and in letters of blood the world would record upon the history of the 20th century a crime unparalleled in all the ages of man.

That hostile army has visited our shores and is now ruthlessly destroying our children.

It is the army of ignorance, indifference, complacency, selfishness and passion. The crowds in the market place, in the cars, on the street, in the theatre give no thought to the waste of life going on around them. They do not see it.

"With desolation is the earth made desolate because no man thinketh in his heart."

If most of these deaths are preventable and if by teaching the fundamental principles of life to our children at school, to our young men and women, to our young fathers and mothers, we can make this dreadful thing impossible, then, indeed, the remedy concerns us all and our failure to heed the facts, as they stand, puts on the shirt of murder.

Of the total number of deaths, tuberculosis was responsible for more than 80,000. These figures represent the number of those who perished of the disease in that year, not the number of those who were afflicted with it and incapacitated by it.

Sixty-four thousand died of diarrhoea and this number indicates in no manner the number who during the year were stricken with diarrhoea and recovered. It does indicate the prevalence of grave errors of diet.

Between the ages of ten and nineteen years, tuberculosis caused 24.5 per cent of the total deaths. Between the years of twenty and twenty-nine tuberculosis caused 35 per cent of the total deaths and between the years of thirty and thirty-nine tuberculosis caused 28.5 per cent of the total deaths.

Cancer, kidney disease and appendicitis stalk along in menacing dignity as important attendants of the great executioner.

The National Association for the Study and Prevention of Tuberculosis informs us that in the year 1911, $14,500,000 were spent throughout the country in the war against tuberculosis. About the same amount was spent in the year 1910. Of the total sum spent last year, $11,800,000 were spent in the treatment of consumptives in sanitariums and hospitals; the remainder was spent by anti-tuberculosis associations, open-air schools, dispensaries and Boards of Health. New York, Pennsylvania and Massachusetts in 1911 spent nearly $7,000,000 in fighting this disease and in the early part of 1912 State Legislatures and other public bodies appropriated over $10,000,000 to continue the work.

The mission of these relentless figures is to awaken you and to arouse in you an interest in the national health. They show that a little army of noble men and women is fighting out there in the field of sorrow with such poor weapons as they have. This book will throw the light on another weapon.

CHAPTER II.

FIFTEEN MILLION DEFECTIVE CHILDREN.

Two hundred and thirty-five thousand children died in the homes of our nation in one year. But how about the living? When the Reaper, Death, had such a harvest, were not his attendants, Disease and Pain, following in his train?

The evils that brought about the death of more than a quarter of a million delicate children in the United States during a year—what was their effect on children with a little more vigor and vitality? What is the actual condition of the school children of the present day?

All over America and Europe public school children are being examined by physicians in their search for disease.

Half the children in a school in the slums of Leeds were found by Dr. Hall to be suffering from rickets, a result of lime and phosphorus starvation. How came that so? We shall see.

In the Edinburgh school, 40% of the children were found to be suffering with diseases of the ear, a result of general systemic disorder, brought about by insufficient food of the right kind or an abundance of food lacking in nutritive value.

Of 10,500 school children the British Dental Association found 86% suffering from defective teeth, the result of a diet lacking in the mineral elements upon which the bones and teeth depend for their existence.

In the Dundee schools 50% of the children were found to be suffering from defective vision.

In Alameda, California, the Superintendent of Schools says that out of 3600 pupils, more than 300 are afflicted with physical defects, observable even to the layman.

Mayor Fitzgerald of Boston in the month of December, 1911, announced the results of the first three months' work conducted by Dr. William J. Gallivan, Chief of the Division of Child Hygiene of the Boston Board of Health.

The school physicians under Dr. Gallivan examined 42,750 children and only 14,957, a little more than one-third, were found to be in a condition that could be called healthy; 27,795 of the children examined were described as defective.

In this historic center of the learning and culture of the United States, an investigation covering three months discovered among the children of the schools 19,518 cases of defective teeth, 9,738 cases of diseased tonsils, 3,509 cases of skin disease, 575 cases of rickets and 1,611 cases of malnutrition.

The Bureau of Medical Research reports that "in rural as well as in city schools, nearly one in three have trouble with the eyes, nearly one in five are mouth breathers, because of abnormal growths in the air passages, besides many who are obviously predisposed to tuberculosis and nervous trouble."

All these infirmities lower efficiency and for this reason Public School Boards are ordering operations upon some children's throats for adenoids, are correcting defective vision for others, doing dental work, providing nurses, furnishing meals at cost price. A few of them are sending cards of instruction on hygiene and diet to parents.

The charge for all these services is borne by the community. If the work were not done under school directions it apparently would not be done at all. The state in these instances exercises vast and elastic powers in the regulation of public health and education.

The great question is: Why does not the State make an attempt to get at the real cause of diseases and instruct the people how to remove the cause?

Our purpose is to set down in plain words here a number of common but deadly sins of diet, the ignorance or disregard of which can end only in disease. Our object is to put in plain form the principles of life so that they may be understood and heeded by parent and child.

He who would enter a race or struggle in a game of the field must know the rules of the game or suffer defeat. In the study of health and disease the laws of nature are the rules of the game. They are simple laws and easily obeyed, but when we ignore them, the price we pay is death. Few of us give them attention for the reason that we do not know them and make no effort to know them until it is often too late.

"A man is a fool or a physician at forty."

The object of the following pages is to make the boy a physician at ten by making his parents a physician when he is born. The period from his infancy to his "teens" will thus be safeguarded and after that he can face the future with no cry against those who brought him into the world: "Why did you handicap me through your ignorance from the beginning?"

Every household wherein ordinary intelligence abides can co-operate with those forces that are striving to educate the nation to a sense of its duty.

If it can be said that the home is the cradle of the nation, it can be said more truthfully that the pantry is the cradle of the home.

Much will be revealed to you here concerning our crimes against our wheat, corn, rice and barley, against our biscuits, crackers and bread, against our canned vegetables and fruits, against our molasses, condiments and sweets, against most of the things we eat, but we shall not destroy without building up. If you would know the truth, told here in all its shocking entirety and help in the work of atonement read patiently the following pages.

The few chapters which are devoted to a description of the building of a human body out of its food are necessary. Their careful reading will prepare you for a complete grasp of all that follows including the chapter on how to feed the child. That chapter does not follow immediately because it is in reality the summing up and interpretation of the hundred food truths that must be understood thoroughly before intelligent provision for the child's food-needs is possible.

CHAPTER III.

DUST THOU ART—NEW LIGHT ON AN OLD TRUTH.

Man has not probed into the real meaning of the words, "Dust thou art and unto dust thou shalt return." Our knowledge of the first law of life has been lost. Perhaps looking closely we may find a subtler meaning than the.one ordinarily given to the saying of Jehovah God to Adam. We may find that it is a law of life, not of death as we have thought.

Let us look at the soil from which we have sprung. If we take a handful of fertile earth into the laboratory and split it up, we find that it is composed chiefly of sixteen elements. When we analyze the body of a man, we find that it, too, is made up principally of the same sixteen elements. If we take next a handful of wheat, lo! again the very same sixteen elements. This is the clue to the riddle of life.

There never was a human body that did not contain these sixteen substances. Evidently these substances are present as the result of no accident. They are: oxygen, nitrogen, hydrogen, carbon, chlorine, fluorine, iron, phosphorus, calcium, potassium, magnesium, manganese, sodium, sulphur, silica, iodine. The body gets these elements from its food.

These sixteen elements, found in the earth, and in wheat, and in man's own body, have formidable names, but as we eat them every time we eat a grain of whole wheat and are not disturbed unduly over their presence at the dinner table, we do not believe we will have much difficulty in studying them to find out just what they do for us, and how our interference with them results in disease and death.

Soil that will produce vegetation must contain oxygen, nitrogen, hydrogen, carbon, chlorine, fluorine, iron, calcium, phosphorus, potassium, magnesium, manganese, sodium, silica, sulphur and iodine.

These special elements produce crops and without them crops cannot be produced.

Without phosphorus all the other elements are worthless even though they be present abundantly. The science that treats of the life and health of the soil is so conscious of this fact that in order that we may have a supply of phosphorus to put back into the soil, to replace our annual drain upon it, the United States government prohibits the exportation of our limited supply of phosphate rock.

We get nitrogen and potassium and the other elements from many available sources but the amount of phosphorus in the mines and in the land is so easily estimated and so very limited and so positively essential, because there is no known substitute for it, we have had to resort to law in order to save our soil from exhaustion.

The upper crust of the earth, known as soil, averages from six to twelve inches in depth. This thin film of earth containing the vitalizing mineral elements that give us all our vegetation is the cradle of the world. The first seven or eight inches of the virgin top soil of an acre of land weigh about two million pounds. In this top soil there are only about two thousand pounds of phosphorus. Thus we see what a wonderful function it performs in combining with the other elements that support life. One little part of phosphorus in a thousand parts of earth! Think of it! Nature's most profound laws are qualitative, not quantitative.

Phosphorus, in proper combination with all the other fertilizing or life-giving elements of the soil together with scientific cultural methods, means normal crops, means health, buoyancy, and vigor in the animal life that feeds upon these crops.

The absence of phosphorus in proper proportion means soil starvation and inevitable loss of vitality.

Science recognizes that this subtle substance, which it has taken hundreds of years to create, must not be removed from the soil if we do not wish the end to come. All the gold and silver and precious stones of the mines, all the piteous cries of starving multitudes cannot recreate this mysterious compounder of life. So science warns us against our prodigality and tells us that if we wantonly destroy it or remove it from the earth or from our food we must pay the price in death.

The laws that must be enacted to conserve the fertility of the earth will make it a crime to destroy the straw-stacks and rough forage that should be used to bed the stables and pens where stock is fed so that it can be burned and returned to the soil in the form of ash to add its mineral fertility to the exhausted land. In the milling districts of the west the straw-stacks are often burned and as their smoke rises heavenward it obscures the light of the sun, symbolizing the darkness under which a wasteful and prodigal people wantonly destroy the elements that give them their life's blood. The life-giving ash is not conserved.

However, phosphorus is only one of the mineral elements, without which life on the surface of the world would become extinct. But, because the available supply of phosphorus is so small, it possesses picturesque importance as an illustration of the necessity of minerals not only in the land, in the vegetable and fruit and grain which the land yields, but also in the life-processes of man and animal.

Iron, potassium, calcium, sulphur, silica, chlorine and the other elements are as important as phosphorus, and when we remove any one of them from the earth, we produce soil-sickness and the fruits of the soil are dwarfed or do not appear at all.

"Dust thou art and unto dust thou shalt return" is a profound utterance containing a great lesson which the twentieth century must learn.

CHAPTER IV.

WHAT THE DUST, OR MINERALS, DO.

We have said that a handful of fertile earth, a handful of wheat, and the body of man, each contains about sixteen elements. Our purpose will be to show the relationship of these elements to life.

Like the blood, the gastric juice, the pancreatic juice, the saliva, the bile and other vital fluids of the body are composed of mineral salts in solution.

It is evident that the mineral salts in the fluids of the body are not there through accident.

Water forms about three-fourths of the adult body and is the medium in which the chemical changes of the body are carried on.

We could transfer an iron tank filled with pure sulphuric acid from San Francisco to New York and back again and the acid would not effect the tank in any manner. If we introduced water into that tank the acid would immediately become very active and destroy the tank. Thus you see that even water is a wonderful medium through which to convey the forces of nature.

We can believe, therefore, that the body of a man weighing a hundred and sixty pounds, made up of more than a hundred pounds of water, contains all that water as the result of no accident.

Of the solid matter to be found in the human body about one-fifth is made up of the minerals— iron, calcium, phosphorus, potassium, magnesium, sodium, sulphur, etc. Chlorides and phosphates with carbonates and sulphates form the chief of these mineral salts. What do they do for us?

If we put a trace of blood under the microscope we discover a wonderful sight. Hundreds of little corpuscles are seen swimming about. Most of them are red, but a considerable number are white. Each has its own work to do.

A single drop of blood contains many millions of corpuscles, far more than all the visible stars in the sky. These corpuscles are not the only things found in the blood. In addition to them we find many mineral salts such as iron, calcium, phosphorus, sodium, potassium, magnesium, sulphur, chlorine, etc. These substances are always found when pure and normal blood is examined, so it is evident that they must get into the blood through some definite channel and in obedience to some well defined law. The red and white corpuscles have certain well defined work to do. It is also evident that anything which interferes with their work or that keeps them out of the blood is an enemy of life.

To make that blood nature obtains her building materials from food. All food contains some of these building materials. Some food contains all of them, except in such instances where man ignorantly removes them. If by accident, we should for a few months consume food deficient in some of these building materials we would quickly feel the effects, in our general health. It is easy to understand that if we are partial to a particular kind of food from which a considerable proportion of nature's building materials have been extracted, we are going to develop disorder.

When the laws under which nature operates are suspended, nature simply does not operate. Man might as well expect a jeweler to make a watch without the materials from which the wheels and springs and screws and bearings are made as to expect nature to make a drop of normal blood without the elements that enter into the composition of blood.

Nature will set up a warning for us before fatal damage has been done, but if we do not understand the warning and do not heed it, we head straight for destruction, unless, in the meantime, some accidental change of diet provides the body with the elements it needs in order to maintain its balance.

Our food is the most important thing in life because upon it all other things depend. We digest and assimilate that food in obedience to a fixed law. If we keep well without knowing that law we are fortunate. It is evident that we should make an effort to locate that law, understand it and apply it.

Each little drop of pure blood is an expression of that law. Anything that interferes with the purity and character of the blood is an enemy of life. Because man leaves everything to chance and as a rule refuses to accept the idea that it is necessary to pay attention to his diet, he sends a call into the unknown darkness and demands hundreds of diseases to come forth from nothingness to assist him in managing the world.

If we remove one element of the necessary sixteen from the food we introduce the beginning of disaster into the body.

If two elements are removed the body may make use of the other fourteen for a time, but soon the unnatural condition under which nature is thus forced to operate will assert itself and disaster will follow.

If three or four or five substances are removed from the building materials, the inevitable collapse will take place a little sooner. If seven or eight elements are removed destruction is speedy. When all sixteen substances are removed starvation begins at once.

Thus we see that the matter of breakfast, dinner and supper, is not a matter to be left to accident or to an untrained kitchen drudge or to a food factory concerned chiefly in the profit-paying characteristics of its products.

If we are pale or anæmic; if our energy seems to be exhausted; if we feel little like undertaking the commonplace duties of the day; if our children have lusterless eyes, pinched cheeks, underdeveloped limbs or abnormal tendencies, let us look to our food. If our children are bright, sturdy and resist disease by not falling victims to the ills which it is wrongfully assumed must come to all children, let us congratulate ourselves upon the lucky accident that has for a time brought to them a supply of the building materials necessary to their development.

In congratulating ourselves let us understand the facts.

An apple falls from the branch of an apple tree to the earth in obedience to a fixed law. A bullet leaves the mouth of a gun in obedience to a fixed law. Rain and snow fall from the clouds to the earth under fixed conditions and in obedience to fixed laws.

If our children are well to-day as the result of the operation of a law concerning which we know nothing, it is necessary to learn something of that law in order that we may consider to-morrow.

The child is well as the result of happy accident. Let us keep him well by understanding the law by which he continues well. The sixteen elements are part of that law.

The body gets these elements from its food and from no other source.

These substances must be in the food in order that the body may take them from the food.

We will now try to find out what these substances do and why they are necessary and how many of them are artificially removed from our most familiar foods without our knowledge, and through our study find the law that will keep us well.

The sodium found so extensively in the blood is found to perform a remarkable function in the processes of digestion. Without sodium, digestion cannot be carried on.

That is evidently part of the law because it always operates in the same way.

Without sodium, we cannot live.

Potassium gives life to the nervous system and assists the heart to beat by influencing the relaxibility or resiliency of the muscles. The heart is a great pump and if it did not send the blood into the lungs the body could not obtain the oxygen necessary to its life. Potassium destroys the hardening influences that menace muscle, joint and artery. It makes the tissues soft and pliable.

Linen made from flax grown on granite soil rich in potassium is noted for its suppleness and softness, whereas linen produced from calcareous soils is hard, brittle and of little strength.

When the body cannot get the quantity of potassium necessary to carry on its wonderfully complex duties, the heart ceases to serve its master, the body dies.

Here is a little laboratory experiment, which

will assist us to grasp an idea of the work which the minerals perform in the human body.

Eat a tablet of citrate of lithium. Take a clean platinum wire, hold it in a blue Bunsen flame. Note that it gives no coloration to the flame. Now pass the platinum wire along the skin of your forehead, or across your palm, return it to the flame, and note the beautiful yellow flame of sodium, showing this mineral in the elimination processes of the body.

Now take a blue glass, and look through it on the platinum wire in the flame, and note the beautiful lilac flame of potassium, showing this mineral also at work in the elimination processes of the body.

Potassium keeps the tissues flexible and active, and assists the sodium to carry off the carbonic gas, manufactured as one of the end-products of combustion in the furnaces of life.

Now about one-half hour after eating the citrate of lithium tablet, again clean the platinum wire thoroughly. Pass it over the forehead, or across the palm of the hand. Put the wire into the flame, and behold the vivid red flame of lithium. In one short half hour, the lithium taken through the mouth, has circulated through all the avenues, highways and byways of the human body, and has appeared in its marvelous journey on the surface of the skin.

Through this little experiment we get an idea of the hidden forces at work in our bodies. As a rule we give no thought to these forces and so are rarely prompted to question the character of this or that food although these forces are derived from food alone.

Those little soldiers that we have called corpuscles are never out of the presence of iron. Containing no iron themselves, they nevertheless float in a fluid which does contain iron and if the iron were not there, the little soldiers would die.

Iron combines with oxygen no matter where we find it.

The blade of a pocket knife is "rusty" or the hinge on a barn door is "rusty" or a rifle barrel is "rusty," and rust is simply a combination of iron and oxygen.

This wonderful affinity of oxygen for iron is part of the law under whose operation oxygen gets into our bodies. Without the iron in the blood we could not get oxygen and in a few minutes we would be dead.

If we choke a man or woman for two minutes, shutting off the oxygen, we are guilty of murder.

Oxygen is so necessary to life that we perish the moment it is taken from us. If the blood contains only half of the iron necessary to bring into the body all the oxygen required, the body from its diminished oxygen supply will grow pale and sicken. Iron is absolutely necessary. It is part of the law.

The waste matter which is accumulating in our tissues during every second of our existence would kill us in twenty-four hours if it were not rendered harmless and carried away. When only partially removed the result is dyspepsia, diabetes, rheumatism, etc.

The iron in the blood uniting with the oxygen in the lungs carries its life-giving freight to the tissues where it oxydizes or burns up the waste substances so dangerous to life.

If the iron is not present in sufficient quantity to keep up with the demands of the body, a large quantity of oxygen that ought to be inside the body doing its work will remain outside the body ready and willing to work but unable to get in.

When fire with the aid of oxygen attacks a piece of wood it produces smoke and ashes. The oxygen-burned waste-products in the body have to be carried away just as the smoke of the fire has to be carried off through the chimney and the ashes raked off through the bars of the grate.

The oxydizing processes going on in the tissues produce carbonic gas. This gas is taken up by the sodium and discharged through the lungs as carbon dioxide.

The sodium besides having work of its own to do has to help the oxygen and the oxygen has to be helped by the iron.

These substances work not singly and alone but in beautiful order and in perfect harmony with each other.

Meat is not wholly a godsend to the man who eats much of it for the reason that it is deficient in the mineral salts which the body requires. In consequence, he who eats meat to excess is plagued with rheumatism, asthma and corpulency and is sent to the mineral springs in order that he may drink water containing calcium, magnesium and sodium sulphate.

Calcium, assisted by phosphorus, magnesium, silica and fluorine, builds up our bones and teeth. Fluorine is found in the whites of our eyes.

If we reduce the quantity of calcium needed by the body in constructing its bones and teeth, we do just what the house-maker does when he uses insufficient material with which to build.

The body makes a poor job of its work just as the house-builder makes a poor house.

Children have defective teeth because they are not supplied with sufficient calcium-phosphate and calcium carbonate or because when these substances are really present in their food, they eat other food that destroys them and removes them from the body.

Fluorine is prescribed in numerous diseases of the eye as fluoride of calcium. Chickens get the fluorine required for the production of their eggs if they have a chance to pick up little specks of granite. When confined in a wooden hen house and fed on food containing no fluorine they easily develop chicken cholera and chicken diphtheria. The yolk of the egg requires fluorine. The enamel of the teeth requires fluorine. The bones of the spine require fluorine. The pupil of the eye requires fluorine.

When the farmer's fertilizer contains no fluorine his cereals and vegetables suffer. The old curse of nitrate fertilizer compels our nation to support a standing army of dentists, but it has not yet inspired us with the knowledge that would prevent curvature of the spine among children.

Silica possesses powerful antiseptic properties. It helps the body to defend itself against the invasion of disease-breeding bacteria. Silica also influences the nervous system to do its proper work in the body. Accompanied with sulphur, it has much to do with the development and health of the hair.

Animals which are fed upon foods from which any of these substances are artificially removed, die.

These minerals not only themselves engage in the construction processes going on constantly within our bodies, but they also exercise a controlling influence over the destructive influences that threaten us from within and without.

The smallest boy in the laboratory can be made to understand the wonderful oxydizing properties of sulphuric acid. When this acid is generated in the body, though small in quantity, if its generation be continued systematically, even for a short time, its results can end only in disaster.

A few drops of it taken into the body from a bottle will produce death.

If food, from which the minerals have been removed, is introduced into the body it results in the formation in the intestines of free sulphuric acid from the albumenoid sulphur.

The sulphuric acid abstracts basic elements from the intestines and tissues, thereby impairing or destroying them.

Meat, which is minced and immersed for a few hours in cold, distilled water, loses its phosphorus and potassium salts. It also loses its color. If cooked in this condition it will be found to be tasteless. If fed to dogs and cats these animals will eat a little, then refuse to take more and if fed on nothing else, they will actually die quicker than animals not fed at all. This can be accounted for not only by the generation of free sulphuric acid in the body of the animals, but also by another fact.

The animals fed on the demineralized meat in addition to being deprived of substances that will sustain life are obliged to dissipate their reserve vitality at a rapid rate through the efforts of their organs to throw off the useless food imposed upon them, whereas the animal that is being starved outright is not called upon to expend its strength faster than the simple laws of starvation demand.

The first part of the law which we are endeavoring to establish is that these mineral substances are so important in our body that when deprived of them we suffer disease or death.

It follows that we must see to it that our food contains them.

There are some dietitians who declare that our food contains an excess of mineral salts. This is sometimes true, but it is as it should be. There is much evidence to indicate that frequently the excess of salts may be carried out of the body in life's processes faster than they are taken in the food without any consequent evil results.

Nature has provided a reserve store-house from which in emergencies the body may find the elements it needs, but if our diet is of a kind that exhausts nature's store-house, we face the consequences that inevitably follow the violation of any of nature's laws.

This fact must be remembered in the feeding of children because when the food of the infant is changed from a purely milk diet to a mixture diet great injury may result through a deficiency of lime salts.

A purely flesh diet, for example, is poor in lime and many of the foods on which children are fed have half the lime removed from them before they are put upon the table. Elsewhere, baby's diet based on the importance of its mineral content will be carefully outlined, also the diet of baby's mother.

Spring time is the season of high spirits in nature. Man alone in the spring complains of lassitude. All around him under the action of nature's unmolested law he witnesses the miracle of rising sap, the quickening strength that swells the bud, the impelling energy that forces the spear of grass to lift itself upward through the lately frozen clod. Man contrasts his weariness with the power and mastery, the sparkle and glow, the warmth and surge and buoyancy of spring, yet just as the earth has the green grass in its depths so has he the freshness of nature in his heart. He is just as much a part of nature. Nature's laws grip him just as tightly in their grasp. He needs his "tonic," or thinks he does, because unlike nature he does not follow the laws of life but closes his eyes upon them and sets up standards of his own. Unhappily his standards are at war with heaven and so he pays his price in death.

Little Helen would be in her mother's arms to-day, strong, bright, happy, if ——!

The mortality records compiled by the census director at Washington, D. C., for 1910, showing that during that year 235,262 children under ten years of age died in the United States, force us to realize that as a nation we have been busier building tunnels, subways, railroads, skyscrapers, bridges, air-craft and Atlantic liners, and living in luxury than in developing healthy, normal bodies.

The time has come when we must teach the child that if he wishes to live and grow strong and be useful, he must eat the foods God has made necessary for the growth of his body.

CHAPTER V.

FERMENTS.

In the bodies of animals and plants these sixteen elements are built up into highly complex combinations and as they are being built up they are also being broken down.

As the tissue is destroyed by daily wear and tear, it is transformed into simpler chemical compounds and passed out of the body. In order that the living body may replace its broken-down cells, it must find a constant new supply of the elements from which those cells are evolved.

These elements as we find them in the soil can be called non-living matter. The chemical processes which transform this non-living matter into living tissues are the same in plants and animals with this one mark of distinction.

Plants are capable of taking the non-living matter from the earth and compounding it into the wonderfully complex substances which form their structure. Animals do not possess this power. Animals are dependent for their existence upon food-stuffs prepared from the non-living matter of earth by the plants that have the power to prepare them. Plants obtain the energy which enables them to do this mysterious work from the sunlight and only in the presence of sunlight can they carry on the up-building processes which give them their tissues. Green grass will not grow in the dark.

We know that under the influence of sunlight, plants are capable of combining the carbonic gas and nitrogen of the air with water and the mineral salts of the soil into such substances as starch, fat and albumen. Their ability to bring about these changes depends upon the presence of a chemical substance which is found in their green parts and which is called chlorophyl.

We know that chlorophyl requires exposure to the sun's rays in order to perform its mysterious work, but of the processes by which it does that work we know little. We know that various parts of the plant and various organs of the body contain substances that can be extracted. These substances are called enzymes or ferments, such as pepsin, trypsin, ptyalin.

These ferments are found in the grains, also in the saliva and digestive juices of the body.

We know that in the human body they serve the purpose of assisting to transform the various foodstuffs which are furnished to the animal by the plant into substances that can be absorbed and built up into animal tissue.

Ordinary baker's yeast is a ferment having the power to transform starch and sugar into alcohol evolving at the same time a waste product in the form of gas. So there is nothing difficult in the consideration of ferments except to keep them alive. That we kill them in our food with "harmless" preservatives or remove them by mechanical means will be shown as we proceed.

It was thought at one time that the ferments found in the digestive glands were the only ferments to be found in the animal body. Accordingly our knowledge of their conduct in the processes of digestion was limited. It has been determined in recent years that ferments are of many kinds and they are present in every cell and are intimately concerned in all the manifestations of life.

As many as a dozen different ferments have been found for example, in the liver-cell. It has also been demonstrated that for the maintenance of life in the case of the higher plants, the organized ferments are of profound importance.

Through them the higher plants obtain their nitrogen in a form which they can subsequently utilize. So even in the presence of all the necessary minerals or mineral salts if these ferments be absent or dstroyed or enfeebled vegetable or animal life cannot exist.

In the animal body some of these ferments such as pepsin, can act to advantage only under an acid condition; while others, such as ptyalin, require an alkaline condition; still others can act under acid, alkaline or neutral conditions. Fixed laws control them. Certain ferments will act only upon certain definite substances and under the proper conditions. We trifle with those conditions at our peril. In its proper place, later on, the geranium of little Helen will tell us much.

Fat-splitting ferments, for instance, will act only upon fats, diastase ferments will act only upon starch and sugar, proteolytic ferments will act only upon albumens.

Of their chemical composition little is known that is definite. We do know that food of the wrong kind, food badly prepared, food which has suffered an unnatural loss of some of its elements can set up conditions that are hostile to the action of these ferments, and that in setting up these conditions, we are inviting physiological discord, which means disease.

It is imperative that we do not interfere with the normal conditions that control the conduct of these ferments. All this will be explained so simply that we will doubtless wonder why we ever tolerated the food conditions that are here described.

We know that human gastric juice is acid in action, the results of the presence of free hydrochloric acid, that it contains sodium chloride, calcium chloride, potassium chloride, magnesium phosphate and iron and depends on these elements for its existence. We know if we remove any of these elements or change any of them or prevent the body from finding any of them, by removing them from our food, we establish unnatural conditions in the gastric juice and immediately bring about disorder.

We know that the pancreatic juice is alkaline in action and contains sodium chloride, potassium chloride, phosphate of magnesium, and lime. From this we learn that one part of the digestion is carried on in an acid medium while another part of it is carried on in an alkaline medium and our conception of the intricacies of the human laboratory increases in admiration and amazement.

It becomes evident in the contemplation of these mysteries that man has no right to ignore the wonderfully complicated structure of his body when he decides that he shall go into business and manufacture foods for the human species.

These enzymes or ferments have such a profound influence upon digestion and assimilation that we receive a shock when we learn that in the preparation of our food we destroy them or change their nature artificially.

These mineral salts and ferments,—let us put it bluntly and nakedly,—are removed from our diet by commercial practices that pander to our false taste-standards and those who remove them have succeeded, to some extent at least, in establishing scientific justification for their work and are able at this stage of the world's enlightenment to fog the atmosphere quite enough to cloud any attempted work of reform under the darkness of controversy.

Chemists and pathologists are to be found who are willing to go on record with some such statements as these:

"Of the metabolism of foods, of chemical change, of the exact action of enzymes and bacteria, we are profoundly ignorant, therefore we should not give much consideration to the mineral content of our diet."

"We get so many minerals in so many articles of food that we can afford to remove most of them from our diet, and, anyhow, so little is known about the conduct of these minerals when ingested with food that the subject is at least not important enough to occasion grave alarm."

Signed statements such as these in spite of such cases as that of little Helen and her 235,262 companions constitute the defense of those whose food industries would suffer if the people enacted state and national laws that would forbid men to denature their food supply.

For reasons of their own some men tell us that if we have enough carbohydrates, protein and fats, bread, meat and butter, we need not bother about the minerals or ferments of our food.

CHAPTER VI.

WHAT HAPPENS WHEN THESE MINERALS ARE LOST OR CHANGED BY CHEMISTS?

The history of life on the surface of the earth is the history of food. Nature builds the bodies of men from food. If certain sixteen elements are necessary in food to build up our bodies, and we remove one or more elements, we invite decay and disease into the body. All food contains some of these building materials; other food—at least as the Creator made it—contain all of them. Sometimes man heedlessly removes some of these elements, leaving the food poorer as building material.

Thus we see that the menu card of breakfast, dinner and supper, is not a matter to be left to accident or to an ignorant kitchen-drudge or to a food-factory concerned chiefly in the profit-paying characteristics of its products.

We have seen that phosphorus is so necessary to the life of the soil that the United States Government has forbidden the exportation of any of our limited supply of phosphate rock. If the one part of phosphorus in one thousand parts of earth in normal farm land is removed from the soil we have a crop failure. If any other of the mineral elements are removed we also have crop failure.

Phosphorus in the soil is no more important than lime or iron, or potassium in the body. We will select lime to illustrate the work which the minerals found in our foods perform in the body.

If we kill a frog and place its still-pulsating heart on a slab of marble, it will be noticed that the frog's heart will not lose a single pulsation for a long time. Eventually, of course, it will collapse and become lifeless. If we wish to prolong its pulsations for many hours, we need only bring it into the presence of a solution of lime.

Under the mysterious influence of this commonest of earths, that dead heart will for hours show all the manifestations of life that might be seen if we could peer into the breast of the living animal.

Lime makes it possible for the digestive ferments to perform their duties.

If we rob our food of its lime digestion cannot go on.

Rennet is a ferment. It is used to make curd from milk. Curd is the first step in the making of cheese. In order that the rennet may do its work it is necessary that the lime in the milk be made soluble and the cheese maker, in order to make it more soluble uses hydrochloric acid.

Tartaric acid or even vinegar would assist in this.

If the lime were not soluble, that is, if it did not enter into solution with a liquid the curd would never become cheese. This is proved by adding a little oxalic acid to the milk while making the curd, or by sterilizing it at the boiling point.

The oxalic acid throws the lime out of solution so that it cannot assist the ferment to do its work and the ferment, deprived of the help of lime, refuses to perform its duty and the cheese is not made.

If you should cut your finger the soluble lime in the blood causes it to coagulate and you do not bleed to death as you would if it were not for this soluble lime in your blood. With a knowledge of these facts we see why lime is so necessary to us. When we diminish its proper quantity in our blood we lower our vitality and destroy our resistance to disease.

The only way we can interfere with the presence of lime in our body is by removing it artificially from our food or by interfering with the ability of our organs to make use of it by eating food of a kind that robs our body of the lime that our food contains.

In every kitchen, restaurant and hotel we are robbing our food not only of its lime but of many of its other mineral salts through our ignorant methods of cookery, and before our food has reached the kitchen we have permitted the manufacturer to rob it of a large quantity of its priceless mineral salts.

When we study the records of defective teeth among school children we face only the surface symptom of much deeper ravages that are going on within the body unseen and unsuspected.

Dr. James R. Mitchell, Lecturer in Chemistry at Forth Worth University Medical College, declares that 86% of the school children of Louisville have badly decayed teeth in spite of the fact that they live in the Lime Stone State!

Doctor Mitchell has pointed out how our dentists prescribe tooth washes and tooth pastes; how they advocate oral hygiene; how they fill cavities and fit bridges, and all the time ignore the fact that the great cause of tooth destruction is to be found in lime and phosphorus starvation.

Some dentists tell us that the sugar we take into our mouth in the shape of candies acts directly and destroyingly upon our teeth. They shut their eyes to the fact that destruction starts first in the pulp of the teeth beneath the surface enamel.

The vital processes of the body can not be carried on without lime. Consequently, if there is a deficiency of lime salts in the food, the body actually begins to tear down its own structure in order to obtain this necessary mineral.

It burrows into the only available source of lime supply, the soluble lime of the teeth and bones and gradually consumes that lime until, in the teeth, it leaves only a shell of enamel over the cavity.

. The enamel sooner or later cracks and breaks under the strain and the damage is discovered. The ruin was accomplished long before we had any evidence of it, although the opening up of an avenue for the entrance of bacteria from without hastens the decay.

Sugar and fruit acids have no effect on the enamel of the teeth. Sound teeth can be immersed in a solution of such acids and sugars for months and suffer no erosion. The sugar does not act directly on the teeth and the dentist treats the symptom, not the cause of our bone destruction.

Sugar and lime have just as remarkable an affinity for each other as the iron and oxygen which we have described, so that when we consume an excess of mineral hungry sweets the sugar with irresistible thirst drinks up the soluble lime of the blood stream and the blood retaliates by sapping the soluble lime from the teeth and bones.

Druggists know how wonderfully lime combines with sugar and accordingly they make what is known as Syrup of Lime. One thousand parts of water will take up one part of lime, but if we add sugar to the water, it will take up thirty-five times as much lime-

Our children will suffer and our prospective mothers will suffer, if they get an excess of refined or denatured sugar in their diet or if our food industries continue to remove the soluble minerals from the chief source of our food supply.

We advance step by step in our study of the indispensable minerals of our food supply and as we advance we must bravely face the great cause of our infant mortality, the great cause of our pale and anaemic women, the great cause of our nervous and unfit men. We must continue to advance until the simple remedy for many of our infirmities is laid bare.

Big butcher shops grind the bones of the ox or sheep or hog into what they call "chicken-bone." If we do not feed our chickens a plentiful supply of lime in the shape of such "chicken-bone" or in the shape of cracked oyster shells or some similar lime food, they will lay soft-shelled eggs.

The dog which is not fed bones will have bad teeth. His skin will be tettered, his hair will fall out and his disposition will be cross. The lioness that is fed with meat alone and no lime in the shape of bones will bear cubs with cleft palates.

Caged mice fed on processed corn meal and distilled water will get "nerves" just as men and women robbed of their lime will get "nerves." As the lime-free diet is continued the mice will be stricken with convulsions.

In the laboratory when pneumonia germs are studied it has been shown that when a stationary growth has been reached a little sprinkle of lime will revive the culture.

Lime is necessary for the strength of the bones, for the hardness of the teeth, for the firmness of the muscles, for the tone of the nerves, for the coagula-

tion of the blood on demand, for every pulsation of
the heart, for the digestion of our food, for the functioning of the kidneys and other vital organs, for the
health of the body.

When a baby is improperly weaned and deprived
of its necessary lime, its bones will be softened and
it will develop rickets. The muscle that is deprived
of its lime will quiver and twitch. The nerve will
do the same.

We know how oxalic acid acts on the lime of the
body when introduced with food.

Food manufacturers who use other chemicals do
not know how those chemicals interfere with the
mysterious processes of life. They say that many
food chemicals are "harmless" and some scientists
are found to agree with them.

But the fact remains that there is premature and
untimely death everywhere. Is it unscientific to
connect these deaths with the follies of our diet system? We leave that to you. One fact remains.

This is now true: In the gradual breaking down
of the food laws for which Doctor Wiley devoted
twenty-nine years of his life, there are nearly twenty
drugs which can be legally put into our "pure" food
supply and there are twelve necessary elements
which can be legally taken out of our "pure" food
supply.

Such facts are eloquent of commercial ignorance
or guilt.

The childish appetite of little Helen for "innocent" cakes, "innocent" candy, "innocent" crackers,
"innocent" white bread, led her gradually and insid-
iously to the hour when her resistance to death was
no longer equal to the pressure and with her Two
Hundred Thirty-five Thousand, Two Hundred and
Sixty-two companions she went on her way to give

testimony to the ignorance of those whose love for her was as high as the hills and as deep as the seas, but whose light through which to express that love was as dark as the night.

Those who raise fancy poultry for the poultry show or prize chickens for the country fair know how to feed their animals according to rigid dietary laws. In consequence, we smile at the very thought of the farmer mixing with his carefully and scientifically prepared food, red, blue, green, yellow, brown, purple or any of the legal coal-tar dyes, borax, sulphurous acid, saccharin, sodium benzoate, sulphate of copper, aluminum sulphate, butyric ether, amyl ether, ethyl ether, oenanthic ether, valerianate ether, formic ether benzoic ether, acetic ether, etc.

All these drugs are now legal with the exception of borax and saccharin.

Although they are legal, the man who has his money invested in raising prize animals refuses to color and drug the food upon which they depend for their prize-taking qualities. Little pigs are tenderly cared for. So are the young horse and the baby calf and wee chicks.

Caution, vigilance, common-sense, scientific knowledge are required and exercised to produce stock that will yield a profit.

In consequence when we invest our money in animals we feed them on a "balanced" diet and the young animals do not die when their food is of a proper kind.

But human beings! That is another matter.

We make the law say: "Thou shalt not buy carbolic acid, arsenic, opium, cocaine, unless the law's restrictions are removed by trained and licensed physicians."

Then we practically say: "Thy food may be whatsoever the food panderer provides."

Now let us tell you the startling fact that the white bread of America is a human destroyer.

If you will read on we will now show you how your daily bread is being robbed of its vitalizing mineral elements and ferments.

Then we will tell you how to go about the work of getting your share of straightforward, honest foods, such as nature provides for you.

CHAPTER VII.

WHITE BREAD STARVATION.

Three times each day, for three hundred and sixty-five days in a year, the housewife in each of the twenty million households in the United States spreads a table with food for the pleasure and nutrition of her family. How many times is that? Answer, you of a mathematical turn of mind! And each one of those billions of times—at least the exceptions are too few to count—the housewife places one article of food on the table, whether in a mansion or a hovel, whether the tables be loaded with the luxuries of life, or whether this be well-nigh the only article of food on the board. Is it to be wondered at, that we call bread the "staff of life"?

But what if the staff on which one leans be broken? What of the man's progress, then? Let us look at a few things about our modern bread.

The flour advertisements in the newspapers and publications tell us peculiar and wonderful things. Hundreds of thousands of dollars are spent to tell us that our flour is washed, brushed, scoured, screened and sifted through silk so that we get utterly perfect flour!

Hundreds of thousands of dollars are spent to exploit anemic crackers, biscuits, cakes and our devoted, solicitous mothers, believing these advertisements, feed these wonderful units of denatured nutrition to their babes and rear a race of such vigor that it sends in one year two hundred thirty-five thousand two hundred and sixty-two of its little ones under ten years of age where white bread and chalky biscuits are needed no more!

Nature never made a white grain of wheat, and man never made a white loaf of bread until about one hundred years ago in the city of London, when an idle epicure conceived the fetching idea of startling his guests with bread as white and lifeless as the aristocratic cloth on which it was served.

The original grain of wheat contains, in organic form, all of the twelve mineral substances needed by the animal body. Chickens, guinea pigs or monkeys fed on whole wheat bread will thrive, but chickens, guinea pigs or monkeys fed on an exclusive white bread diet will die.

How does the white bread get white? White bread gets white because from the ground grain of wheat three-fourths of the minerals, including the phosphorus, iron, lime, chlorine, silica, sulphur, potassium and magnesium are removed.

These elements are contained in the brown outer skin of the wheat berry, called the bran, and in the "shorts," "middlings," and "tailings," which are sifted and bolted out of the ground meal, leaving principally the white starchy part of the interior part of the berry.

Nature in her divine effort to teach us that we cannot interfere with the laws of life through thousands of years of agricultural experience has failed to teach us the priceless value of these subtle substances which she goes through so many divers ways to assemble for our needs.

Not alone are the minerals removed, but one of the wheat's ferments, discovered by M. Mege Mouries in the inner cortical part of the wheat is rejected in the fine white flour. Its function when introduced into the body is not fully known, but as it is one of the things which we thoughtlessly destroy, we mention it here.

Those who make our flour and our bread for us think they can "prove" that they are conferring a great blessing upon humanity in giving us the refined white product with which those slaughtered innocents were so familiar and when we raise a cry of protest against their "proofs" they laugh and show us the signatures of chemists.

What chemist's signature will open up those little graves and deliver back to the fond and empty arms of grieving parents the million children that have died in this country during the past four years?

The millers admit that they do not give the people white flour or white bread through their own choice, but that because the people think they want white flour and white bread they are obliged to pander to them.

If we take an animal membrane, a bladder, and fill it with a solution of any mineral and hang it up, there will be no leakage through the skin; not a drop will appear on the outside of the bladder. We can let the solution remain in the bladder for days and it will guard its contents as safely as a glass bottle.

If we now take the filled bladder and immerse it in another solution of different density or of different kind, the contents of the bladder will immediately begin to pass out through the walls of the bladder into the solution on the outside of the bladder, while the solution on the outside will pass through the bladder membrane into the inside, so that eventually we will find the solution on the outside and the solution on the inside exactly the same in character.

The dissimilar liquids are now thoroughly diffused. This is called osmosis. It might also be called life. Osmosis is going on in the body all the time.

We recreate the mineral constituency of the blood every time we eat and thereby we keep changing the character of the fluid on the outside of the cells in order to keep it different from the fluid inside so that osmosis during life never ceases.

In fevers, accompanied by extreme exhaustion as the result of inability to consume food, or in cases of starvation, the fluids inside the cells and outside the cells gradually become identical in quality so that osmosis becomes very feeble and almost ceases. When it ceases altogether death arrives.

The minerals which nature put into our wheat and which we so deliberately remove are lost to us forever and the vitalizing missions which they would have naturally and beneficently performed are never performed at all.

Hundreds of tons of these "useless" bi-products are annually removed and devoted to purposes for which they were never intended. More of this later.

This debauching has been going on now for a century and yet we stand in stupid bewilderment before the advancing scourge of tuberculosis.

We cannot seem to understand that we are deliberately reducing our national vitality by every ounce of organic mineral salts that we take out of our food and destroy.

Then as to the bran sifted out of the flour some millers say that the silica which the wheat berry contains is practically "ground glass" and he cautions us against feeding "ground glass" to our tender babes.

They should also say that because wheat contains iron, it contains horse-shoes; that because it contains lime, it contains bone dust or white-wash; that because it contains magnesium, it contains face powder that because it contains phosphorus, it contains match heads; that because it contains fluorine, it contains the enamel of human teeth and the whites of human eyeballs; that because it contains chlorine, it contains bleaching compound; that because it contains sulphur, it contains the flames of Hades.

There are many prejudices to overcome in restoring whole wheat products and whole wheat bread with all their wealth of vitality to the people. The "ground glass" idea will probably meet with the sympathy of many doomed souls who are reluctant to give up their sickly loaf.

Some of the millers say that this "ground glass" contained in the bran of the wheat is an irritant and that, therefore, people not in normal health cannot use it without injury.

Some "Science Notes" fell into our hands in the month of December, 1911, stating that an "English Commission," but not mentioning what kind of an "English Commission," has been looking into the subject of bread and that it finds the presence of bran in the use of whole wheat to be advantageous in special cases, but that in general, it is an undesirable element in bread because it is itself indigestible and interferes with the digestion of other nutritious factors in the food.

Of couse, it is indigestible in the sense that in its course through the body it is not taken up by the body and transformed into tissue.

We do not digest pepper, nutmeg, cinnamon or any other spices. Ground spices, like ground bran, contain much indigestible fibre but this fibre contains valuable properties, the influence of which upon the digestive processes is well known.

The miller who through his solicitude for our welfare would not permit us to eat whole wheat says nothing about our consumption of pepper, cinnamon, nutmeg or ginger.

We all know that the seeds of strawberries, raspberries, figs and grapes are indigestible, yet no being discards the seeds out of strawberries, raspberries or figs before eating these luscious offerings of mother nature.

The millers in their consternation at the thought of our eating the bran of the wheat fail to warn us against eating corn on the cob. Every time we eat a "roasting ear" we eat the "bran" of the corn and every time we eat beans or peas, we eat the "bran" of the bean and the "bran" of the pea and it is well that we eat these things, because while they are not digested in themselves, they surrender to the body the invaluable mineral salts which they contain. Accordingly, while it may appear to the dullard that they have no place in the diet of man, they contribute wonderfully to the life-giving properties of his food.

Just as chopped meat surrenders its mineral salts to the water in which it is immersed, through the processes of osmosis that we have described, so also does the bran of the wheat surrender its minerals to the body in the same way. But—the bran not only furnishes indispensable mineral salts to the body, but its chief virtue is as a regulator of the persistaltic action of the alimentary tract by which its contents are kept moving onward.

One of the curses which white bread, or robbed bread, has inflicted on the people is constipation. A thousand ills are traceable to this disorder.

Read the patent medicine ads to get an idea of how many thousands of people require "pills."

Inhibited peristalsis is the malevolent origin of the woes of so many American women who are afflicted with uterine and ovarian diseases.

Bread made of the whole wheat just as it comes from nature, together with the other reforms for which these pages cry out, will save our daughters and our daughters' children from the evils which food follies have imposed upon them.

In Dr. Albert Westlake's new edition of his book on "Babies' Teeth to the Twelfth Year," he says:

"Babies' teeth should receive consideration at least six months before the child is born. Necessary elements in their building up are furnished at this period by the mother's blood, hence, the need of the purity of the latter.

"Teeth require more organic phosphate (particularly phosphate of calcium and carbonates of lime) than other parts of the body; therefore, bone food is necessary for the mother (cow's milk, eggs, especially yolks, peas, beans, lentils, WHOLE WHEAT, OUTER GRAINS, etc.)

"Dietetic treatment for the mother is very important at this period while bone is forming.

"The intestines of the child are also undergoing vital changes at this period and earlier. This includes the primary fixation of the child's intestine in the left hypochondriac region.

"It is, therefore, vital to the offspring to get perfect peristalsis of the mother's intestines. Elimination and evacuation should be regular WITHOUT DRUGS."

For this reason alone, the mother should not be robbed of the potassium, sodium, magnesium, iron, phosphorus, sulphur, silica and chlorine which the honest wheat affords.

The millers will never know how many babies they have handicapped by their disregard of the laws of nature or by their assumption that they know more than nature may teach.

No chemist can tell us in terms of grams anything about the exact quantity of phosphorus, iron, potassium, lime, silica or chlorine which we should take into our bodies every day. Nature has fixed that mysterious and hidden thing for us. Confounded in our wisdom, we turn our backs and seek a new way through the dark.

The chemist admits he can never tell us that, and three chemists at Columbia University devoted months to a study of three of these minerals, determining nothing as to the quantity of them required, but determining everything as to their necessity.

The millers and bread makers do not know the trail of wreckage which they have left in the wake of their mineral contempt. They do not know how they have burrowed into the vitality of human life while it is still in the mother's womb. They do not know to what extent they have been responsible for tuberculosis, diphtheria, pneumonia, scrofula, measles, scarlatina, anæmia, etc.

If we could stop at this point and launch in the same manner our indictment against barley, rice, oats, corn, many prepared cereals and many breakfast foods, all of them with a few lonely exceptions being robbed as wheat is robbed, we would achieve our goal of putting you on guard against the food crimes of the nation and show you how to prevent those crimes but we would go no faster than we are going now. Read carefully and you will learn.

The crime of denaturing our food begins with wheat and we will stick to wheat and "wheat products" until we have made it clear that we are to continue our journey downward into an abyss of national degeneracy if we do not stop and make such soundings as will tell us where we are.

Normally healthy lungs give an acid reaction with litmus paper. This acid has been found to be phosphoric acid. It is present in the lecithin of the lung tissues.

In tuberculosis the lungs give a neutral or alkaline reaction with litmus paper due to the absence of phosphoric acid.

In all cases of tuberculosis of the lungs a deposit of lime is found. Sometimes this deposit is very slight but as the disease makes headway it becomes so great that the anatomist has to deal with what is called "the chalky lung."

It would be impossible for this lime to be deposited in the lung tissues if the phosphoric acid of the lecithin in those tissues was normal.

Chemistry, so far, has not established a final anaylsis of lecithin. Lecithin is a phosphoric compound of the body. Nuclein, however, which is another phosphoric compound of the same importance is found to vary, depending upon the health of the individual, between 2.5 per cent and 9.5 per cent in its phosphorus content.

The blood of a human being containing as little as 2.5 per cent of phosphorus in its nuclein substance shows a quantity just as deficient in the lecithin of the lung.

On the contrary, where the blood of a vigorous body shows the maximum of 9.5 per cent of phosphorus in its total mineral content, the lungs show an equally high percentage of this mysterious element and it is always found in the form of phosphoric acid.

As you decrease the phosphoric acid in the lungs, you increase the lime deposit. As you increase the lime deposit you prepare an alkaline field where the germ of tuberculosis may take root and grow.

As you phosphorize the blood you render it capable of supporting the nutrition of the lung tissues and as the lung is kept in health, it is protected against the invasion of tuberculosis.

We cannot go into a theater, a church, a crowded street car or walk along the dusty city street without inhaling the living micro-organisms which cause tuberculosis, but if our lungs contain their normal quantity of phosphoric acid, we need have no fear because the germs are destroyed as fast as they enter our bodies.

If this were not so, everybody would be stricken at the same time with tuberculosis and nobody would resist the disease.

It is the same with typhoid fever. In cases of typhoid epidemic, there are some who do not get the disease. They do not get it because their vitality is so normal that it resists the diseases. The absence of a proper supply of phosphorus in the blood is due to an insufficient supply of phosphorus in the substances taken as food.

Let it be remembered that from the hundreds of thousands of bushels of wheat "milled" every year in the United States, from the hundreds of thousands of bags of rice "polished" every year in the United States, from the tons and tons of barley "pearled" every year in the United States, from the enormous quantity of oats soaked, scoured, bleached and "prepared" every year in the United States, from the thousands of barrels of corn ground every year in the United States, the phosphorus is removed. We have seen what takes place when we remove phosphorus from the soil and we are now beholding the tragedy that is being enacted under our eyes as we remove phosphorus from our bread and from our bodies. More than half of the insane are consumptives. A peculiar fact has been noted in connection with the bones of the insane. They are very brittle and easily broken. This brittleness is due to phosphorus starvation. Where calcium phosphate is present in normal quantity the bone is tough and resilient.

Remember three-fourths of these substances are removed from our daily bread.

CHAPTER VIII.

POLISHED RICE.

As we gather up the shattered fragments of the broken statue that once stood so brave, so eminent and so long unmolested before the pale ignorance of the white wheat eater, we may catch in fancy the murmur of spirit voices, among them, little Helen's voice, saying: "We, the ghosts of little children, are patrolling the night pulling down from their high niches of darkness whatsoever symbols of disease and death we find. Yonder a skinny finger beckons. It is the finger of bloodless fraud. Pull it down, its name is Polished Rice."

Few Americans have ever eaten rice as nature intended them to eat it. The beautiful grain, midway between cream color and light brown in hue, with a flavor that the polished rice eater has never tasted, has been banished from the United States for many years.

The robbed substitute is the brushed, scoured, polished and talcum coated grain of commerce so degraded and denatured by the processes through which it passes that if fed to the fowls of the barn yard they will die when given no other food. If fed on the natural grain containing all the elements which nature placed in it they will thrive.

The "innocent" bowl of rice as we now scour and polish it served to the growing child and the convalescent struggling desperately upward out of the snare of disease, will not support life. We have robbed it as we rob the wheat.

Not the cry of the alarmist, this! Behold the facts.

In the Philippine Islands they have a disease which they call beri-beri. We have similar diseases in the United States but we call them inanition, anæmia, neurasthenia, nervous prostration, paralysis, death.

Beri-beri journeys from one stage to another through all of these experiences.

Its name neither adds to its ability to kill nor detracts from its ability to kill. Those who get it die the death.

Dr. V. G. Heiser in the year 1910, then Director of Health of the Philippine Islands, Doctor Fraser of Singapore, Dr. Aron of the Philippine Medical School, Dr. Highet of Siam, Dr. DeHaan of Java, produced evidence that showed conclusively that beri-beri is caused by a diet of polished rice such as is exclusively consumed in the United States.

The polished rice does not introduce some mysterious germ into the body. It simply starves the blood and tissues until they no longer offer a defense to the germ, and then it takes up its seat in the weakened body and develops.

Some chickens were fed with polished rice and others with natural brown rice. As has been here set down the birds fed on polished rice died, the others thrived.

In the months of January and February, 1910, there was a severe outbreak of beri-beri among the inmates of the Culion Leper Colony which resisted all treatment.

Then all polished rice was discontinued and the natural grain substituted. The sick in the hospital were treated with rice polishings. Rice polishings contain the phosphorus compounds and other mineral salts, ferments and nitrogenous products which are brushed, scoured and polished off the grain in order to make it white for the delicate eyes of pale women and children to glory in, for not in wisdom but in glory do they eat.

A few months' diet of the natural grain to which the rice polishings had been added brought about complete cures and stopped the spread of the disease. Yet little Helen could not find a pound not even a short-weight pound of that natural brown rice in all the land.

Science needed more evidence to convince it that man had no right to denature his food.

So. Dr, Fraser, in the Straits Settlements, and Dr. Aron of the Philippine Medical School set about to prove that when we brush, scour and polish away the phosphorus compounds and other organic minerals that are present in the pericarp of natural rice we rob the human organism of its requisite supply of these elements.

After this fact had been demonstrated to the satisfaction of the physicians in the far east, it was again experimentally confirmed in chickens and later in human beings by feeding polished and unpolished rice to a group of railway workers in the Straits Settlements.

The Quarterly Report of the Bureau of Health of the Philippine Islands for the first quarter, 1910, says:

"The group of men that partook of the No. 1 polished white Siam rice developed beri-beri within a period of approximately sixty days while the group that partook of the unpolished

rice remained free of the disease. Every effort was made by interchange of clothing, by
contact and by living in the same house to convey the disease to the group that ate of the
unpolished rice but not a single case developed.
The process was then reversed. The group that
partook of the polished rice was changed to
the unpolished rice and vice-versa and within
a period of approximately sixty days the group
partaking of the polished rice developed beri-
beri. These experiments were further confirmed in Manila by the use of rice polishings
in the treatment of beri-beri patients who
showed immediate improvement in their condition and except when the disease was too far
advanced promptly recovered. In view of the
apparently certain evidence upon which the
etiology of the disease now rests a recommen-
dation has been made to the Governor-General
of the Philippine Islands to forbid the use of
polished rice in public institutions. It is hoped
by this means not only to eradicate the disease
from such places, but also that it may serve
as an educational factor in disseminating knowledge as to the method by which beri-beri may
be avoided."

The Governor-General issued an executive order
on June 3, 1910, to all health officers and presidents
throughout the island, forbidding the use of polished
rice in all government workshops, prisons, hospitals
and other institutions and directing the officials having control of such institutions to see that the
provisions of this edict were complied with at once.
Polished rice was bad food in the Philippines but
elsewhere people could do with it as they wished.

In the meantime China and Japan have both taken action against "robbed" rice by denying it a place in the diet of their soldiers and sailors.

Under date of October 27, 1910, the ever-vigilant Doctor Harvey W. Wiley, writing from the Bureau of Chemistry, Washington, D. C., to the writer, said:

"While beri-beri is not a disease common to this country, perhaps, due to the fact that our diet is not composed exclusively, or almost exclusively, of rice, yet it seems to me we should not even in a small way permit a condition of nutrition which would favor the development of such a disease as beri-beri or some other disorder due to the debasement of rice from polishing. Rice is becoming a more general diet in this country and the dealer who first begins the campaign for a pure, unadulterated rice will surely promote the cause in a commercial way which will do much toward protecting the health of the people."

Physiologists recognize that organic compounds of phosphorus are absolutely necessary to the health and well being of man. This fact is balanced by another fact of startling importance. Man, unlike the plant, is unable to manufacture his own organic compounds of phosphorus from inorganic phosphorus.

Doctor Alexander Bryce of Birmingham, England, goes as far as to declare that "it is even probable that a daily supply of the different compounds of organic phosphorus is necessary in the food, as no proof exists to show that nucleins, lecithins, phosphatides or phytins are capable of being substituted one for the other."

We know that beri-beri owes its origin to a deficiency of the organic compounds of phosphorus.

Schaumann has shown that polished rice which introduces tropical beri-beri or even the ship variety of beri-beri which arises among the European crews of sailing vessels forced to live on food largely deprived of its organic phosphorus, will also produce polyneuritis in fowls. Schaumann proved that barley and white wheat flour can induce the same disease. He also showed that by demineralizing foodstuffs of any kind through the action of solvents or by high temperature the same disease can be induced

It has also been shown that physicians cannot supplement the mineral deficiency of food with organic or inorganic phosphates. The patient under such treatment will die just as quickly as he would under no treatment at all. But food products rich in organic compounds of phosphorus such as peas, beans, wheat bran, barley polishings, rice polishings, corn phytin (the parts of the grains which are removed in milling) when added to the demineralized or defective foodstuffs are capable of preventing the development of the disease and can cure it when present. These organic carriers of phosphorus must be present with the other food in sufficient quantities to supply at least two grams of phosphorus per day, that being the minimum amount required for an adult.

Remember that beri-beri is simply an extreme state of mineral starvation. Between perfect health and beri-beri there are a hundred mile posts each one representing another by-post into the barren desert of disease or death.

The necessity of phosphorus in the human organism and the necessity of administering it in such an organized form that it is capable of being assimilated has been proved.

Despite the establishment of this fact, terrible and tremendous in its significance, we carelessly destroy the organized minerals for which surgeon and physician even at the uttermost extremity of death can find no substitute.

CHAPTER IX.

A statement made by Dr. Frederick Gowland Hopkins, Fellow of the Royal Society, Reader in Chemical Physiology, University of Cambridge and an investigator of European fame, was sent to the writer by Miss May Yates, Founder and Honorable Secretary of the Bread and Food Reform League of England, in the month of May, 1912.

"The superior value," says Doctor Hopkins, "of whole wheat meal lies in the fact that it retains certain, at present, unrecognized food substances, perhaps in very minute quantities whose presence allows our systems to make full use of the tissue-building elements of the grain. These substances of undetermined nature are apparently removed to a great extent from fine white flour in the milling.

"I began long ago a series of experiments on the relative tissue-building values of fine white flour and of flour which contains a large proportion of the whole grain. These experiments were made among others in the endeavor to discover the nature of the unknown substances which I have just mentioned. In their existence I believe greatly because of my experimental results."

Doctor Hopkins experimented with an eighty per cent whole wheat meal which though not containing all of the wheat yet had a much larger proportion of the grain than does white flour. Even with such material his results were remarkable as will be seen. His conclusions are:

"All my work to date confirms my belief in the superior food value of standard whole wheat bread. After definitely proving that young animals grow with very much greater rapidity on brown flour than on white flour, I have been able to improve the tissue-building rate of the white flour subjects, by adding to their white flour an extract made from the brown flour. To make the best use of any food material such as the proteins, etc., certain other food substances, and possibly a variety of them must also be present in definite proportions.

"If one essential food constituent which ought to make up say even as little as one per cent of the total food is present in only half its normal amount, then when it is a case of building up the tissues, the system will only be able to make use of half of the other food elements, even if these other elements make up the main bulk of the food."

At this point Dr. Hopkins reaches the most significant paragraph of his statement. Here are his words:

"This principle has long been recognized as regards plant life and growth. A plant, in order to attain perfect growth, must find in the soil a certain minimum of each of many elements. Consider, for example, the element potassium. Suppose only half of the necessary amount of potassium be present, then no matter how abundant may be all the other soil and air constituents, their normal utilization is limited to one half. The rate of growth and the ultimate development of the plant are consequently depressed.

"The absolute amount of potassium employed in growth is very small compared, say, with the carbon or nitrogen; but any deficiency in it limits growth as surely as a deficiency in the more important elements. The substance of unknown nature which I just now mentioned may need to be present in very small amount but if the necessary minimum is not available, the utilization, in tissue growth or repair, of all other constituents is infallibly deficient. In the process of converting the wheat grain to the fine white flour these unknown elements are lost or destroyed to a great extent. It follows that no matter how much iron, phosphorus, etc., may be retained in the white flour our systems cannot make the best use of them."

In addition to Dr. Hopkin's statement, Miss Yates supplied the writer with a statement signed by Dr. E. S. Eddie and Dr. G. C. Simpson, confirmed by Professor Benjamin Moore, professor of bio-chemistry at the University of Liverpool, offering further irrefutable evidence of the essential health-giving qualities of the bran of the wheat grain discarded in milling white flour.

Doctors Eddie and Simpson are members of the research staff of the School of Tropical Medicine, University of Liverpool.

"It has been proved by Braddon and other workers in the East that exclusive use of polished rice as a diet leads to a form of periphernal neuritis. This disease does not occur in those native races who use whole rice as a diet. Our own experiments have been extended to similar work in relation to the stripping of the outer case from the wheat berry so as to produce a white bread instead of a whole or standard bread and we find that parallel results are often obtained when the outer layers are excluded from the diet with both wheat and rice. These experiments clearly demonstrate that the outer part of the grain contains the essential constituents for the nutrition of the nervous system both in growing animals and in adults."

(Signed)   E. S. EDDIE.
(Signed)   G. C. SIMPSON.

The following are some of the details of the research work now being carried out with standard and white breads in the bio-chemical department of the Liverpool School of Tropical Medicine by Professor Benjamin Moore, Chief of the Department:

"Groups of pigeons have been fed on fine white bread made from white flour guaranteed to be unbleached and unadulterated, while similar groups of pigeons have been given an ordinary quality of standard whole wheat bread bought from a regular baker. The white bread pigeons have all speedily developed marked symptoms of ill-nutrition and serious nerve derangements. Besides losing weight they sit listless and shivering, lose power in their legs, suggesting nerve paralysis, while many develop convulsions.

"The standard bread pigeons on the other hand, keep healthy and up to normal weight.

"In another series of experiments pigeons which had developed grave nervous symptoms on such diet recovered completely when after a week of special nursing they were placed on an exclusive standard bread diet during their convalescence.

"All the recent work done in our bio-chemical laboratories proves beyond question that in all cereals, such as wheat, barley, oats and rice, there are series of important substances incorporated in the inner layer of the husk which are essential to the nutritive value of the grain. If these elements are eliminated in the milling or preparation of the grain, a diet largely composed of cereals or bread thus denatured will not only fail adequately to nourish the body, but will tend to set up active disease.

"Certain of the diseases of mal-nutrition among children, notably rickets, scurvy-rickets, tetany and convulsions present symptoms very similar to those we note in our white bread pigeons. So striking is this similarity that physicians who have followed up our work are already treating certain of their scurvy-ricket patients with a diet of standard bread.

"Our nerves as a nation are much less stable than in the days prior to white bread diet. All our work suggests that the growing tendency of the age to neurasthenia, 'nerves,' ets., is not unlikely due to removing from our diet those very elements of cereal foods which nature has hid in the husk of the grain and which man in his ignorance discards."

(Signed) DR. BENJAMIN MOORE.

The letter with which Miss May Yates accompanied the above statement is as follows:

THE EDUCATIONAL HEALTH AND FOOD CAMPAIGN
INAUGURATED AT

THE MANSION HOUSE

UNDER THE PATRONAGE OF H. R. H. THE PRINCESS
CHRISTIAN, BY

THE BREAD AND FOOD REFORM LEAGUE.

(A purely uncommercial, educational and non-political association.) Supported by The National League for Physical Education and Improvement. The Royal Institute of Public Health, The National Conference on Infantile Mortality, The Social Institute's Union, The Children's Protection League, The Mothers' Union, etc.

"Although an act has been passed dealing with the feeding of school children, it does not touch children who are WRONGLY FED, and who, through ignorance, are handicapped for life, mentally and physically, by scanty or improper feeding.

"As prevention is better than cure, a knowledge of the right selection and proper preparation of food is of vital interest to all classes of society, for a deficient supply of materials to form muscles, bones, teeth, brains and nerves is most injurious to the health, stamina and welfare of the rising generation."

Headquarters: 5, Clements Inn,
Strand, London, W. C.
May 3, 1912.

Dear Sir:—

As my attention has been directed to a controversy that you have held with the American Miller on the subject of Whole Meal Bread, I venture to send you the report of our Bread and Food Reform League, the report of some physiological experiments showing the superiority of brown whole meal and cream colored bread over the very white bread in general use.

You will also find a summary of papers on the same subject that I read at the Portsmouth meeting of the British Association and the Health Congress of the Royal Institute of Public Health.

Hoping these papers will interest you, believe me,
                              Yours truly,
          (Signed)   MAY YATES, Hon. Sec.
Alfred W. McCann, Esq.

CHAPTER X.

PROPER FOOD OR MEDICINE.

In March, 1912, Dr. Armand Gautier addressed an audience in Paris. He declared that man in the course of his evolution had lost the instinct of nourishing himself. Eating has thus become an art which has to be learned by man, while the lower animals when left to themselves have an innate knowledge of the proper food. It is absolutely necessary that mankind possess a certain amount of scientific knowledge in order that we may choose our proper diet.

Man has indeed lost the instinct that the beast still possesses. That instinct would enable him to select, as the beast selects, the food that would prevent disease, but man has been given intelligence and will with which to select his food. The choice should not be turned over to an ignorant kitchen drudge.

Food underlies all art, all progress, all peace, all happiness; it underlies the existence and safety of the world.

"We must curtail our waste of food products in the home, on the farm and in transit, for every pound of food that is produced is needed, as fully one-half of the people in the world go to bed hungry every night," declared Colonel Henry Exall, president of the Texas Industrial Congress of Dallas. "The lofty human thought that suggested the means to bring together the august ambassadors of

all the nations in conference at The Hague," he
continued, "to form compacts for international and
permanent peace is worthy of the most exalted praise
of this enlightened age, and God forbid that its edicts
should not be perpetual and everlasting; but I warn
you that no parchment yet manufactured will be
strong enough to make a treaty binding against a
cry for bread."

We know that nature obtains her building materials from food. All food contains some of these
building materials. Some food contains all of
them, except where man ignorantly removes them.
If we for a few months eat food deficient in some of
these building materials we quickly feel the effects
in our general health.

When the laws under which nature operates are
suspended, she simply does not operate. Man might
as well expect a jeweler to make a watch without
the materials from which the wheels and springs
and screws are made as to expect nature to make a
drop of normal blood without the elements that enter
into the composition of blood.

Our food is the most important thing in life because upon it all other things depend. We digest
and assimilate that food in obedience to fixed laws.
If we keep well without knowing those laws we are
fortunate. It is evident that we should make an
effort to understand and apply them. We have great
need to look well to the sources of our food supply.

The cow that is fed on the denatured waste
product of the cotton-seed oil industry of the south,
or the demineralized brewer's grain, or corn-oil-
cake and similar debased cattle foods, cannot furnish
us a proper supply of milk.

The cow that is given a normal oxygen supply
and fed on natural grains and on the grass of the

field is, like the horse, free from tuberculosis. The cow is fed for milk production. The horse is fed for vitality and breeding.

As a result practically no horse can be found afflicted with tuberculosis, whereas almost half of the cows of the States of New Jersey and New York are 'so afflicted. This seems to be a sweeping statement yet it is absolutely true. The milkman will not give his new-born calf the milk from its tuberculosis mother, yet he is not always so particular about the new born babe of the human family. He has no money invested in the latter!

Not only is there a deficiency of phosphoric acid in the lungs of the tuberculous but there is the same deficiency in the milk of tuberculous cows.

Milk is produced in the tissues, not from the food direct. The milk of the cow cannot be healthy unless its tissues are healthy.

Just as tuberculous lungs give a neutral or alkaline reaction with litmas paper, so does the milk of tuberculous cows contain an excess of the alkaline minerals. An alkaline field is necessary for the growth of disease-breeding bacteria.

The percentage of phosphoric acid in cow's milk is found to vary between ten per cent and fifty per cent of its total mineral content. Some milk is so poor in phosphorus that its caseine can be analyzed without showing a trace of this mineral.

Let us not forget the difference in the health of human beings, the mineral content of whose blood shows 2.5 per cent of phosphorus and those whose blood shows 9.5 per cent.

Analysis also shows that some milk is ten times as rich in iron as other milk. One per cent of the minerals of some milk is iron, whereas, but one-tenth of one per cent of the minerals of other milk is iron. No wonder infants die!

A large portion of cow's milk is of poor quality, low in phosphorus, low in iron.

You ought to know whether the milk on which your child is fed contains the least possible quantity of phosphorus and iron or the greatest possible quantity. If your infant is fed on milk containing ten per cent of phosphorus and one-tenth of one per cent of iron, and your neighbor's infant is fed on milk containing fifty per cent of phosphorus and one per cent of iron, you can tell which infant is most likely to live.

In 1910 there were 19,000 children who died in New York City under two years old, and 15,000 of them were less than a year old. The Health Commissioner roused by these facts began looking after the city's milk supply. Among other things he opened fifteen stations where infants' supplies can be had and instruction is given in the care and feeding of babies. This work is as yet barely begun, but in 1911 the deaths under two years had dropped from 19,269 to 17,574.

Love is sometimes a matter of phosphorus and iron.

When the child leaves the milk stage again it is necessary to see that its iron and phosphorus are not interfered with. Love will be awake and see to that. Ignorance will sleep as before. Love blesses; ignorance kills. The laws of life are fixed. Why give the child normal milk for the first two years of its life and put it on denatured grains thereafter? Healthy and normal milk for its first two years and after that healthy and normal grains, vegetables and fruits, and above all, honest and normal bread will save your child.

One of the arguments that the defenders of white bread advance is that people do not live on bread alone; they eat other things.

The children of the poor live largely on bread, and if it is an honest loaf of bread made from honest wheat grown out of honestly nurtured soil, there is no necessity for anxiety with regard to health, even if for a time there is bread alone to eat.

Such bread will support life and if, for a time, no other article of food were present the child would have a life-sustaining meal.

But if that bread has been debased and denatured, there is nothing else for the spirit of justice to do but to cry to heaven for vengeance.

The well fed business man who eats a great variety of food and whose digestion is good will not fade and die simply because he eats white bread. He runs a good chance through his generous diet of getting most of his body-requirements, but his wife who stays at home and her children with their bread and coffee for breakfast and their "hurry-up" luncheon from the "delicatessen store," they are the first victims.

Even the vegetables cooked at home are largely denatured, as the soluble mineral salts which they contain are thrown down the waste pipe with the water in which the cooking is done.

We know that the phosphorus, potassium and iron of the body are at war with the germs of tuberculosis to say nothing of other disease-breeding germs. Metchnikoff describes the white corpuscles of the blood-stream as defenders of the body against disease through their power to destroy disease-breeding bacteria. This power he attributes to the organic phosphorus compound of the white corpuscles which the scientist calls nuclein. When these phosphorus compounds are normal in the body invading bacteria are destroyed as fast as they enter. When the defending army of phosphorus is weak, the invading bacteria take possession and triumph.

In the meantime are not we making the defending army as weak as possible by removing the phosphorus, iron and potassium from the most of the food we eat?

Every time we boil a potato and throw away the water in which it is boiled we throw away potassium. Every time we make a white flour from the grain of wheat or send a bag of polished rice to the market place or a carton of pearled barley to the grocery store or a sack of corn meal to the kitchen or a carton of scoured oats to the pantry or a package of bi-product breakfast food to the morning meal of our children, we are doing our best to starve the defending army of phosphorus and make it possible for the powers of darkness and disease to triumph.

If phosphorus and iron and potassium and the other minerals which we have been considering are so necessary, why does the physician not give us a bottle containing them and let us put them back into our own bodies after we have taken them from our foods?

The physician tries to do just that. He has his iron tonics and his phosphorus tonics and his potassium iodides, but they do not get into the body as they ought. Because these minerals must be organized as they are organized in nature before the human body can make proper use of them.

You will remember that we showed you that a mysterious substance known as chlorophyl enabled the plant to take these non-living or inert minerals from mother earth and transform them into its tissues. You then probably asked the question: "What has all this got to do with me or with this subject?"

We have reached the explanation.

The human body does not possess the power that the plant possesses through its chlorophyl to appropriate these minerals to its needs and it must, therefore, depend upon the plant which has that power in order to obtain in an organized and assimilable form the elements on which it depends.

If this were not so we could go direct to the stone pile or bed of earth and eat clay, for the clay contains the elements of life.

It is through his food that man must get these minerals, hence iron, phosphorus, potassium, etc., in the form of drugs do not cure tuberculosis or any other disease.

The physicians who used to study only drugs and symptoms will now study and prescribe foods, foods, foods. The despised Italian fruit-vender at the street corner is a noble American institution. By his display of greens and fruits, he constantly tempts mineral-starved bodies to eat these raw and life-giving carriers of mineral salts. No one knows what a blessing the Italian has brought into this hurried, unthinking, ignorant land through his fruit stand.

Grains and fruits and vegetables have the power of picking up the various necessary minerals from mother earth and forming them into the complex organic compounds ready for animal life to assimilate.   .

This book may not oblige people to heed the light. But there are many afflicted people in the world who murmur: "How is it possible that there can be a merciful or a loving God when he so scourges the earth with sickness?" To these in particular is this chapter addressed.

"As we sow, so shall we reap." As we prepare the way for disease so shall we suffer disease. If we gratify every whim of our palates, if we eat with the eye rather than with the intelligence, we cannot at the same time blame God for sickness. The folly is with ourselves and with our wayward, selfish, unthinking habits of life.

The great obstacle in the way of reform is the housewife's desires. She wants unnatural colors and characteristics, not thinking or not knowing that these defeat the purpose for which she buys food.

She wants yellow butter, artifically colored with a mineral or so-called vegetable dye, though she is satisfied to have a white Swiss cheese which is the natural color of the milk from which butter and cheese are made.

She wants white bread and white rice but doesn't ask for white oatmeal.

She asks for bleached apricots, bleached peaches, bleached apples and bleached pears from the dried fruit family, but she is satisfied to have her raisins and prunes and currants unbleached, almost black.

Her soda biscuits must be the hue of a starched shirt front, but black devil cake and dark brown ginger bread do not frighten her.

Give nature a beautiful color scheme that satisfies the eye, and take from her the elements necessary to build a healthy body and nature will fail.

For our two hundred thirty-five thousand two hundred and sixty-two children under ten years of age who died in one year in these United States, we would not give nature her demands, and nature failed!

Commercial rapacity and dishonesty with the wide freedom it now enjoys through the absence of effective laws that would control its lust for gain, is one of the great enemies in the path of reform.

No sooner had references to the virtues of natural brown rice begun to appear in newspapers and publications, particularly in the editorial columns of Collier's Weekly, than an attempt was made for commercial purposes to deceive the people into believing that the long debased white rice of the market place was really after all the "natural, unpolished rice" which had been made the subject of so much discussion in the medical profession of the Philippines.

Until about a year ago practically all the rice on the market was coated with glucose and talc. Such rice was known as "coated and polished rice," but some of the rice traders conceived the idea that by omitting the glucose and talc, the rice, even though it had been scoured and brushed and robbed, could legitimately masquerade under the title "unpolished." This was assumed evidently on the ground that inasmuch as it had not been polished with furniture oil and a chamois skin it could be truthfully said to be "unpolished."

Accordingly, because the people had never seen the natural brown grain and therefore had no standard by which to make comparison for themselves, a so-called "unpolished rice" appeared and in its advertisements clamored for the faith and favor of the helpless and the weak.

It was the old rice in everything but the veneer of glucose and talc! What of that? Who would know it?

The packages in which it was offered for sale bore such phrases as: "Great Natural Health Food."

"Uncoated and Unpolished." "Recommended by Physicians." "Most Nutritious."

Inside the package an educational slip of paper was introduced which said:

"The treatment of rice, called 'polishing,' to meet the American demand that it look white and glossy removes some of its most valuable properties and is the chief reason why ordinary commercial rice lacks in nutriment as compared with the natural unpolished product eaten by the principal rice consuming nations."

Yes, the advertisement actually condemned the polished rice in these words.

Then followed a chemical analysis of fats, proteins, sugar and starch, leaving the mineral substances strangely out of the tabulation.

To this fraudulent appeal for favor this paragraph was appended:

"The above comparison shows clearly why the average grocery store rice lacks in flavor and food value."

The very wording under which this food product was introduced betrayed the fact that its commercial progenitors knew what they were doing and did not hesitate in such a grave matter, affecting the public health, to exploit impoverished foods as life-savers and body-builders.

For twenty-nine years Doctor Wiley fought the food adulterators, yet in the year of our Lord nineteen hundred and twelve, nearly six years after the Pure Food and Drugs Act of June 30, 1906, became a law, we find such avaricious traders dishonestly using the efforts of reformers, appealing to the ignorance of the public, spragging the wheels of reform, and brazenly administering an antidote for "trade reasons" to the struggling spirit of truth.

Are we content to permit the grasping hands of food panderers to reach into the sacredness of our homes to the destruction of our offspring for the unholy profit which is their god?

Laws are needed, but mightier than laws in bettering the conditions under which humanity lives, is education.

We needed no law to compel us to use the telegraph, the telephone or the electric light when electricity was developed for practical use. Most of us need no laws to keep us from buying poisons. Doctors used to think it was the right thing to bleed their patients, sometimes to death, but we need no laws now to prevent such bleeding.

When the average normal mortal knows what is not good for him, he will usually leave it alone without the interference of a law.

This book attempts to turn on the light and show the facts. The knowledge of the truth will result in the demand of the housewife for honest whole wheat meal from which nothing has been subtracted and to which nothing has been added, so that from it a loaf of life-sustaining bread may be made for her child.

She will demand an honest whole wheat breakfast food ground to the same consistency as the farina and other highly debased breakfast foods with which she is familiar, but unlike such breakfast foods, containing all of the elements that nature put into the wheat.

If she doesn't make her own bread she will demand that the bread of the baker be made from honest whole wheat meal, not a mixture of eighty per cent patent flour and twenty per cent so-called entire wheat flour which is not entire wheat at all.

When Doctor Sylvester Graham advocated the wheat meal that took its name from him and has since been known as "graham flour" he did not advocate the commercial make-shift of modern times that is made by adding thirty-five pounds of bran to one hundred and sixty-one pounds of white flour, producing a barrel of so-called "graham flour" weighing one hundred and ninety-six pounds.

He did not advocate an imitation "graham flour" containing 7 per cent bran instead of 10 per cent; 10 per cent shorts instead of 16 per cent; 5 per cent coarse middlings instead of 14 per cent; 6 per cent fine middlings instead of 16 per cent; 72 per cent of starch instead of the 44 per cent natural to the wheat.

The natural, honest, "graham flour" sells at $5.00 per barrel; the imitation can be prepared from by-products for less than $4.00 per barrel.

The dealer with an extra dollar profit in sight would rather sell the imitation. Everybody is looking for profit. So, quality and honesty suffer and food is juggled.

The housewife will make her biscuits and cakes and crackers from the whole wheat and she will use that meal in making the creams and sauces with which she dresses her intelligently cooked vegetables using the water in which she cooks them.

The little flecks of brown and gold which the honest wheat meal contains add unusual daintiness of appearance to the sauce and the flavor of such sauce can never be appreciated until it has been tasted.

She will demand the natural brown rice even though it requires a little longer time to cook it and she will demand unpearled barley and unsoaked, unscoured, unsteamed, unbleached oatmeal. She will.

demand the old-fashioned, southern stone-ground, undegerminated corn meal made from all of the corn, and when she learns how to make her porridges and her corn cake and her oaten cake and when she sees around her happy, healthy, children with sparkling eyes and well-rounded cheeks and sturdy limbs, she will begin to believe that love is indeed sometimes a matter of phosphorus and iron.

Yellow Corn mugher in U.a.

CHAPTER XI.

MEAT EATING INSUFFICIENT.

Some of you will think that we have omitted to consider one large item of ordinary food, and the meat eater will ask: "But do not I make up in my steaks and chops for what the food industries take from me, and thus is not my diet well balanced?"

No, your meat does not balance your diet. If you did as the meat-eating beast does, and ate the blood and bones of the animal as the dog and tiger and panther do, you would get all the elements of life which the flesh and blood and bones contain, all the phosphates and oxides, all the calcium and iron, all the nitrates and sulphates; but, when we kill our meat-producing animals, we drain them of their blood and throw away their bones, and thus with the exception of nitrogen, potassium and phosphorus, we get little else in our flesh diet but the waste products which at the moment of its death are being developed in the animal's tissues.

It is easy to bring about in young dogs a condition resembling "rickets" in children by feeding them on meat and fat alone. If we add pulverized bone or calcium carbonate to their meat and fat, the animals recover. Undue reliance on your beef or lamb or pork or veal, while it may satisfy the appetite, will not satisfy the body-needs.

We do not agree altogether with those who say that there is no place whatsover for animal flesh in the diet of any man. We know that there are times

when a meat diet seems valuable provided the meat
is taken from a healthy animal and none of its ex-
tractive juices are removed in the cooking.

Yet we should remember that catarrh, rheumatism and blood diseases can never be cured where
meat is consumed more than two or three times a
week and that these diseases are usually associated
with flesh-eaters.

For every pound of beef consumed by man, ten
pounds of corn are necessary to produce that pound
of beef. A pound of beef will support one man for
a given length of time, but the quantity of corn necessary to make that pound of beef would support
more than ten men for the same length of time.

When we eat the flesh of the animal we eat the
end-products of the animal's life processes, urea,
uric acid, etc.; when we eat the grains and legumes,
the nitrogen supply is just as great, even greater,
and without the urea.

The meat eater who demands meat every day
should eat only such meat as was permitted by the
Mosaic law and slaughtered by an orthodox Jew
who believes in that law. So safeguarding his appetite for flesh, he will eat less of the disease-producing
elements found in the animal's blood at the moment
of its death under commercial methods

In his animal chemistry Liebig cites the rest-
lessness and incessant movements of meat-eating
animals, lions, tigers, panthers, hyenas, wolves, and
observes that men who habitually eat meat manifest
similar irritability and lack of repose.

Prof. James Rollins Stonaker of Stanford University, put some rats in rotary cages containing
speedometers that registered the number of miles
traveled by each rat. Some were fed meat and others
only vegetable food. The meat-eating female rat ran

5,447 miles, while in the same time her vegetable-eating sister ran 447. The meat-eating male rat ran 1,447 miles, while the vegetarian ran only 200 miles. But this condition of high pressure in the vital processes is functional excitement not true invigoration. To be stimulated is not to be strengthened and re-created. Look at the larger animals. The panther paces wildly, while the elephant, camel and horse in reposeful strength plod along unexcitedly and when put to work endure as no other animal endures.

An editorial in one of the New York papers commented with mild sarcasm on this rat incident as follows:

"While we have not made such striking experiments, we have noticed these facts ourselves in our observation of the animal kingdom. Take the case of the poor elephant. He does not taste meat in his whole life, being reduced to such miserable fare as shrubs, the tops of bushes and little trees, and other such food lacking in nutrition. As a result the elephant seldom attains a weight of more than 10,000 pounds, and the hardiest specimens do not often live longer than 200 years.

"The rhinoceros, which also has a thin diet much like the elephant's, is notably of poor physique. He is perhaps not more than twenty times as heavy as the meat-eating leopard. His brother the hippopotamus, which grubs around the edges of rivers, is noted for his slim and delicate figure. There, too, is the feeble camel which does not have meat on its bill of fare. It is so lacking in endurance that it cannot pass more than a couple of weeks in the desert without water. No specimen of our Alaskan moose weighing more than 2,500 pounds has yet been found.

"We might cite many other instances, but we do not think that Professor Stonacker's theory needs any more."

A word as to the digestion of meats, which begun in the stomach is completed in the intestines. One-fourth of all the blood in the human organism is in the liver performing its works day and night. One of the duties of the liver is to elaborate the bile. Between two and three pounds of this fluid are secreted by the liver every twenty-four hours. This vital fluid aids in the absorption of fats and checks putrid fermentation. It acts as a natural stimulant of the intestinal mucous membrane. The billary acids are powerful antiseptics. When the bile, through digestive disorders, passes into the stomach it interferes with gastric digestion. When the organs are in normal action it assists in preparing the partially digested food that passes from the stomach into the action of the intestinal juices, thereby fitting it for assimilation into the living organism.

It excretes many of the poisonous decomposition products from the body and if interfered with, these decomposition products accumulate and by auto-intoxication sicken or kill.

Too much meat or too much nitrogenous food of any kind, peas, beans, lentils, cheese, eggs, nuts, require the liver to produce a great quantity of bile in order to work them out of the system.

Most people consume as much energy in getting rid of worthless food as they do in a hard day's labor.

CHAPTER XII.

WHAT WE SHOULD EAT—REAL FOOD.

Millions do not know the taste of meat and when it is known that the vital salts, potassium and phosphorus with negligible traces of iron and calcium, constitute the meagre contribution of meat to the twelve indispensable salts which the body needs, there is abundant reason for not overestimating the value of meat. Many of the races of the world scarcely ever eat meat.

The chief food of the Japanese consists of rice, pulse, sweet potatoes, turnips, carrots, squashes, egg plants, peas, beans, radishes, oranges, peaches, pears, apricots, plums, persimmons, raspberries, bulberries, currants and herbs which they dress in so many different ways.

Are not the Japanese robust, well made, active, healthy, long lived, intelligent? Compare the mortality records of their army with the records of the Russians whom they defeated.

The Greeks eat black bread made of unbolted rye or unbolted wheat meal. With a bunch of grapes, a handful of raisins or figs, this diet keeps the Greek laborers astonishingly athletic and powerful.

The Turks and the people of Malta eat black bread and coarse macaroni supplemented with garden stuff and Sicilian wine, goat's milk, cheese, fish, raisins, ripe olives and other fruits, thistle broth, boiled thistle stalks, dandelion and vegetables.

The diet of the Chinese is practically without meat.

The Russian laborers, millions of them, eat black bread with a bunch of garlic, supplemented with cabbages, mushrooms, vegetables and milk. Those who can afford it have boiled millet pudding, goat's cheese, onions, cake made of unbolted Indian corn, vegetable soup, "black broth" and weak tea.

The Norwegians eat rice, bread, milk, cheese, hasty-pudding, porridge of oat meal or rice meal seasoned with herrings or mackerel.

The Spanish peasant eats unpolished rice, brown bread, grapes, raw onions and drinks light wine.

The French peasant eats dried beans and peas, potatoes, boiled rice, milk, greens, pancake made of wheat meal and eggs, salads, curded milk and little wine or meat is consumed except during the time of hay making and harvest.

The Swiss workman rarely tastes flesh. His food is principally brown bread, cheese, potatoes, vegetables and fruit with large quantities of milk.

The Scotch eat oatmeal, oatmeal cakes, potatoes, milk, butter, bacon, but little other meat.

So let the American race possessing the largest and most varied supply of food of any race on the earth, take that food in its original nutritious state, as furnished by the all-wise Creator.

Let us have unbolted wheat meal containing all of the wheat, nothing added, nothing removed, and natural brown rice, unbrushed, unscoured, unpolished, containing all of the rice, nothing added, nothing removed.

Let us have old-fashioned oat meal with the hull removed by the old dry process, without steam or steam heat. When the oat or any other grain is steamed, some of the soluble mineral salts which it contains are washed out and carried off. When the steam condenses on the surface of the grain and trickles off, it carries with it the vital elements which it holds in solution.

Let us have unpearled barley, a beautiful golden grain, containing all of the barley, nothing added, nothing removed.

Let us have maize meal and corn meal unbolted, ground from the undegerminated corn.

Let us have wheat food or mixtures of wheat and rice or wheat, rice and barley granulated to the same degree in which we usually find the demineralized, denatured, debased farine and similar so-called "breakfast foods."

Let us have the barley loaves of Biblical tradition, the maize loaves of history and the wheaten loaves, the rice cakes and the delicious oat cakes of centuries ago.

Let us have wheat muffins of the whole wheat meal, and date cakes and fig cakes and raisin and prune cakes, the very names of which are no longer known to the refined and exhausted dietary of modern times.

What is true of over-indulgence in nitrogenous food, flesh, peas, beans, lentils, eggs, cheese, nuts, is also true of over-feeding on carbohydrates (sugars and starches). The importance of carbohydrates as food stuff is secondary. They are totally unable to take the place of nitrogenous foods. A definite amount of these nitrogenous foods is necessary that life may be maintained. Starch and sugar do not replace nitrogen. White bread and potatoes are principally starch. Candy is 95 per cent sugar of glucose. White bread, potatoes and sugar are common types of the carbohydrates.

Potatoes should be alternated with other fresh vegetables such as carrots, parsnips, turnips, beets and a dish of steamed natural brown rice or unpearled barley should be frequently substituted for them. With the potato let there always be some of the green vegetables such as cabbage, cauliflower, spinach, brussels sprouts, etc.

Like all the legumes and grains, the pea, bean and lentil contain the mineral salts in different proportions, one being rich in chlorine, another in phosphorus, another in calcium, etc.

The lima bean and navy bean and pea and lentil, are like meat, rich in nitrogen, but with the mineral salts that meat lacks. To cook them, soak them in cold water over night for ten hours at least. Use only such quantity of water as they will absorb. Never throw the excess of water away. It contains the tissue salts that are so valuable. The fireless cooker affords an ideal method of cooking them and they should remain under the action of heat for eight or ten hours.

Beans, peas and lentils contain an average of about twenty-five per cent of proteins, nearly two per cent of fat and about fifty per cent of carbohydrates, sugar and starch. They are rich in potassium, phosphorus, calcium, magnesium and contain traces of iron, sulphur, silica, chlorine and sodium. Of the total mineral content of these three legumes more than one-third is phosphorus and more than one-third potassium. As a base for the principal meals of the day or as an addition in small quantities to the lesser meals, the legumes are valuable, but should not make up more than one-fifth of the total quantity of food consumed.

Lentils are nearly three times as rich as peas and beans in chlorine and about ten times as rich in sodium, but they contain only about one-fourth the quantity of magnesium. They possess four times as much iron as peas and beans, although only traces of sulphur and silica are to be found among them, whereas in peas and beans the sulphur is considerable and the silica quite noticeable. In phosphorus content all three are practically the same.

Peas and beans contain a large quantity of potassium. By having lentils one day, peas the second day and beans the third day, we vary the meals so as to get just what we need in right proportions. Combinations of these legumes can be made flavored with the juice of onions, spinach, cabbage, turnips, parsnips, parsley, celery, etc.

Of the cereals, the oat is the richest in minerals, barley next and wheat third, closely followed by rye, corn and rice. This means the whole grain. In processing, polishing, pearling, bolting, etc., the grains lose more than 75 per cent of their mineral value. Like beans, peas and lentils, the various cereals differ widely in potassium, phosphorus, iron, calcium, etc.

More than half of the mineral content of natural brown rice is phosphorus and nearly half of all the other cereals with the exception of oats is phosphorus, the latter containing but about one-fourth of this element. Whole wheat meal, natural brown rice and undegerminated corn are rich in potassium, and all about equal in iron.

Barley contains lime, calcium and only a trace of chlorine. The breakfast foods made of the whole grains should also be varied so as to balance their mineral gifts.

Among vegetables, spinach is the richest in mineral matter, with cabbage, horse radish, potatoes

and lettuce following close behind. After that we
find carrots, radishes, onions, cauliflower, cucum-
bers, asparagus, etc. The green vegetables are very
low in protein and starch with the exception of potatoes; for this reason they should always accom-
pany the legumes and cereals. Their chief advantage apart from their mineral value is in the necessary bulk they afford to the food. Bulk is required
in order to stimulate peristaltic action and to properly distribute the digested elements so that the processes of assimilation may be carried on gently and
continuously.

In cooking the green vegetables, the water in
which they are cooked should never be thrown away.
With the addition of whole wheat meal and butter a
most delicious sauce can be prepared. By saving
this sauce for the needs of the body instead of for the
waste pipe of the sink, we prevent anemia or mineral
starvation. This liquor also makes delicious soup.

Of the fruits, the dried fig is the richest in mineral matter containing about three times as much of
the organic salts as any of the other fruits. Next
to the fig in mineral value is the blueberry and after
that in close order the strawberry, prune, cherry,
apple, peach, gooseberry, grape, etc.

The potassium content of all fruits, with the exception of strawberries, is high. Figs, strawberries
and apples are rich in sodium. The other fruits with
the exception of the gooseberry, prune and peach
contain little of this element. The apple contains
little calcium; all the other fruits contain a large
quantity of this element. In magnesium there is little difference in the fruits, the fig being richest. The
strawberry, gooseberry and prune contain most iron,
the strawberry, however, being twice as rich in iron
as the prune.

In phosphorus content all the fruits are about the same with the exception of the fig, which contains but a trace of this necessary element. In sulphur there is little difference, it making about one-eighth of the total mineral content of the fruits. The strawberry is very rich in silica. Next to it, a close second, is the cherry. The other fruits contain a small quantity of this element. Those who object to whole wheat bread because of its silica content should not eat strawberries. The chlorine value of fruits is low.

Nuts are extremely rich in minerals, particularly in phosphorus, potassium, magnesium and calcium. The cocoanut contains about six times the quantity of chlorine found in any other nut. The chestnut is very starchy but contains little fat. The other nuts are rich in protein and fat, but contain little starch. The cocoanut is also deficient in protein, whereas the other nuts contain a high protein content.

The egg is rich in sodium, calcium, iron, phosphorus and chlorine. It contains nearly twice the quantity of mineral matter in cow's milk.

A man weighing one hundred and sixty pounds, possesses in his body about forty-five pounds of carbon, fifteen pounds of hydrogen, ninety pounds of oxygen, three and a half pounds of calcium, one and a half pounds of phosphorus, one and a half pounds of chlorine, three and a half ounces of sulphur, three and a half ounces of fluorine, three ounces of potassium, two and a half ounces of sodium, two ounces of magnesium, one and a half ounces of iron, one ounce of silica and one half ounce of manganese. If we do not consume sufficient organic phosphorus, potassium, silica, magnesium, iron, sodium, etc., in our food our body draws upon itself to its own destruction for these necessary elements.

Children must be taught this fundamental truth in order that as they come to maturity they may see the necessity for obeying the laws of life in regard to their food.

CHAPTER XIII.

CANDY, ICE CREAM AND OTHER FOODS.

In considering molasses, let it be understood with a shudder that as now manufactured this popular sweet is enfeebling the stamina of the race. Its curse rests heavily on the head of the child because it is usually consumed with another cursed product, bread.

We must realize that starch, gum, gelatine, glue, mucilage, dextrines and sugars, serve as sources of energy and fat but are not building materials for the tissues of the body.

When starch, sugar, glucose or molasses are not properly combined in the body or are not fully oxidized to carbonic acid and water, as the tissues are broken down, they are excreted in the urine, thereby manifesting in the system, "diabetes mellitus."

Cane sugar acts like an acid, corrosively, upon iron and steel. It also acts upon lead, taking this metal into solution. Confectioners recognize this activity of sugar to such an extent that they employ copper and tin-plate kettles.

Containers and faucets containing lead produce poison where sugar or molasses comes in contact with them. Foil containing lead, used as a wrapper by candy makers, also produces poison.

Like the juice of the maple, the juice of the cane contains iron, calcium, magnesium, phosphorus, silica, etc. The affinity of sugar for lime is shown in the mineral content of the juice, of which nearly one-fifth is calcium oxide.

We thus see how with any "refined" sugar from which the lime and other minerals are driven out the sugar takes on an insatiable hunger for lime, iron, etc. We are thus able to understand how such demineralized sugar attacks the lime and iron of the tissues which in turn attack the lime and iron of the blood, thereby robbing the body of these indispensible substances and preparing it for the invasion of disease.

Raw brown sugar and honest molasses free from sulphuric acid and sulphurous acid would be a blessing, not a curse, because they would give to the body the tissue salts which they possess and thereby save the body from the destructive action of the "refined" product.

Molasses as now prepared has an ugly history, which grows out of our national worship of commercial gods. In the old days the juice of the cane was clarified and evaporated in open kettles set directly over the fire. To-day it is clarified by the use of sulphurous acid which is subsequently neutralized by an alkali. In the process the flavor and aroma are greatly destroyed by the sulphurous taste and odor which remains in the product to injuriously affect the health of the unsuspecting consumer.

In some sugar factories the sulphurous acid is introduced as gas; in others it is introduced in the form of solid acid sulphite of lime. Part of this sulphurous acid is oxidized to sulphuric acid. The ordinary molasses possesses little of the flavor of the old-fashioned open kettle syrup. Instead of the old product, we now have "Refined Molasses." One method of refinement consists in suspending in water acid sulphite of sodium which is brought into contact with zinc dust.

The solution that results from this process is then mixed with the crude molasses.

Molasses is thus bleached or refined and the aroma and flavor which do not escape in the effervescence which follows the mixing, are bound up under the effects of free sulphurous acid.

Sometimes oxalic acid is employed. There is always danger that the resulting "refined molasses" may contain poisonous zinc salts or poisonous oxalic acid salts.

Other methods of bleaching molasses are produced by the action of chloride of tin.

The free sulphurous acid of so-called New Orleans Molasses is liberated when brought into contact with the hydro-chloric acid of the gastric juice. This would be tolerable under a pagan code of morals that gave no value to child-life where the prosperity of great industries was concerned.

Of 18 samples of molasses examined by the Pennsylvania Department of Agriculture in 1912, 14 were found to contain the poisonous metal zinc which probably was introduced into the molasses in the form of a zinc chloride used as a flux for soldering the tin cans in which the molasses was sold.

Of 20 samples analyzed, 18 contained the poisonous salts of tin. All molasses is rich in soluble and insoluble mineral salts, but the vicious contamination with sulphuric acid and sulphurous acid together with traces of zinc and tin makes the modern commercial production of this splendid food product a shameless and unspeakable crime which is justified only on the ground that the national health is of less importance than the national wealth.

Mention is made on the label of the molasses in tin cans that it contains sulphur dioxide. However, this does not take the curse off the molasses, the molasses taffy, the molasses ginger bread or cookies containing it.

We have gone so far astray under the direction of commercial chemistry that nothing but complete revolt will check the evil.

Not even revolt will bring back to the heart of little Helen's mother the sunshine that has gone for her into the shadows forever. In the meantime the extra profit of a penny per quart consoles the conscience of the molasses-maker.

When a State like New York provides for its Department of Agriculture only $10,000 a year with which to enforce the Pure Food Law and permits its legislators to distribute hundreds of thousands as additional salary grabs for political henchmen, it would seem to be time for an accounting to the families doped with food frauds.

New food laws are needed. Funds are needed for their enforcement. Capable chemists and fearless inspectors are needed. A commission, free from commercial taint, for the purpose of establishing food standards is needed. An official authority to determine the harmfulness of certain elements now employed by food industries, and an official power to condemn such elements are needed.

Candy makers in New York State who use shellac in the manufacture of their products, as well as talc and sodium sulphite, can defy the department at Albany to molest them. Under the law as it stands, the candy maker is safe from prosecution.

The cheap candy factory can be classed as an enemy of the public school's efficiency. By its unnatural appeal to childhood's most easily misdirected

impulse it imposes a heavy handicap upon the work
of teaching.

The gravity of this handicap can be measured
by the public's distorted sense of values in estimating
the worthiness of this or that foodstuff. Many of
the worthless food compounds that enjoy the questionable honor of "popularity" among children,
enjoy a deplorably enormous sale.

One stumbles into cheap candy factories and
cheap confectionery stores almost as often as he
passes a saloon or soda water fountain. The cheap
candy factory helps to keep alive the methods of
trickery common to the 15th century when the
Spaniards greedily bartered gaudily colored caps,
brilliantly tinted glass beads, fantastic hawk's bells
and other painted trifles for great quantities of cotton yarn, cassava and small ornaments of gold.

European avarice soon learned that with such
colored appeals it could trade successfully for anything the native possessed. It is the survival of
this method of color appeal which has developed the
trade of the cheap candy factory with the modern
American child to such an alarming magnitude.
Everywhere the child is confronted with artificially
colored sweetmeats. It is taught in its most impres-
sionable years that the greatest appeal is to the eye
and it soon forms the pernicious habit of judging
from the surface instead of from the substance.
Everywhere we hear white-haired wisdom saying:
"The American public loves to be fooled."

The maker of penny candies has discovered that
from the same batch of glucose, often sweetened
with saccharin, he can produce sixty varieties of
colored candy with the aid of permissable coal tar
dyes, to catch the fancy of the passing child.

Even when such candies, contain nothing less wholesome than glucose or nothing more dangerous than saccharin the added color appeal leads its youthful victim into the vicious excesses against which every family physician so repeatedly cautions in vain.

The law which protects child life from many other dangers because of some picturesque touch of horror does not consider that this more subtle and consequently less perceived danger falls within its power. No one in sound mind denies the physical menace of the bad, cheap candies containing paraffin, carpenter's glue, sulphites, soap-stone, shellac, radiator lacquer and coal-tar dyes.

The most innocent of such ingredients is said to be soap-stone, sometimes known as talc, although anyone who has seen the keen, splinter-like spicules of talc under the microscope must know that they have no wholesome function to perform when they become imbedded in the delicate mucous membrane of the child's intestinal tract.

Our purpose is not so much to denounce such dangerous candy as to emphasize the influence of so-called "innocent" candy in perverting the child's processes of judgment and to denounce the unfeeling industry which lives and prospers through its unchallenged system of exploiting the untrained and too often unrestrained appetites of boyhood and girlhood.

In the growing years, the penny candy is often a substitute for nutritious food, too often impairing and destroying the taste for such food.

How many young men of feeble digestion and how many anæmic young women can attribute their physical infirmities to a long continued disregard of the fundamental laws of nutrition brought about through artificially cultivated taste and warped judgment?

The candy factory with its penny product helps to initiate the great vice of food inebriety.

To disorder the senses from early childhood is not a fitting preparation for useful manhood or womanhood. Penny candy has much to answer for.

Glucose at $2.00 per hundred pounds, with the aid of coal-tar dyes, becomes candy worth from $20.00 to $60.00 per hundred pounds. At the time of this writing glucose bleached with sulphurous acid, or unbleached, is worth $1.31 per hundred weight.

Is it upon the unrestricted freedom of such profit-making trade that we build the soundness of American youth? Can it be said that candy of this description contributes in any manner to the welfare of the child?

It is time, indeed, that the mothers of America should formulate laws of their own designed to discourage the tremendous consumption of debased sweets among their children.

Pineapple, strawberry, raspberry, banana, peach, cherry, plum flavorings for candy, pop and soda water are false. No chemist, prior to the year 1912, has ever succeeded in putting on the market a pure fruit extract made of these flavors. No such flavors have ever appeared on the market. Science has not been able to devise a means of capturing the volatile flavors of such fruits. The whole scheme is false, deceptive, misleading.

So-called extract of pineapple used by the candy maker and soda fountain is a mixture of chloroform, amyl oxide of butyric, aldehyde, butyric ether, citric acid, oil of lemon, glycerin and alcohol. This mixture whose destiny is the human stomach is sold under the Pure Food and Drugs Act in the most dignified and thoroughly legal manner.

The invalid who eats a dish of gelatine or the child that drinks a glass of soda water flavored with these chemical triumphs looks into a very appetizing and apparently very innocent delicacy.

Strawberry extract is made of nitric ether, acetic ether, formic ether, butyric ether, amyl oxide of butyric, ground rhatany root and some essential oils and alcohol, a legal compound for the child's soft drink, for the icing of the fancy cake and for the beautifully colored ice cream. There are a few commercial industries engaged in the manufacture of candy, ice cream, soda water, cake, etc., who classify these drugs according to character and will have none of them. Up-to-date, the number is few.

Raspberry extract is another fascinating creation. It is made of nitric ether, aldehyde, acetic ether, formic ether, oenanthic ether, benzoic ether, etc. Raspberry is popular with the child in sweet meats, sweet drinks, sweet cakes and ice cream. Perhaps some of the derelicts who dope themselves in later years with morphine, cocaine and similar consoling agents have cultivated their abnormal appetites in their childhood from some of these foreign substances which they have been able to secure so easily.

Banana extract, cherry extract, plum extract, peach extract, extract of apple and extract of pear are made in the same way with the addition of valerianate ether, valerianate oxide of amyl and acetic oxide of amyl. Is it not remarkable that a form of government so delicately paternal in its functions as to define poisons and prohibit their sales and use, should limit its interest to certain chemicals whose actions are sudden and radical? Poisons are poisons whether they kill in a night or in a thousand nights. The least dangerous poison is the hurry-up kind marked with skull and cross-bones. Such a poison warns us and we can keep away from it.

The most dangerous poisons are the subtler and the slower poisons which in time, undermine the health and by lowering the vitality permit the invasion of disease. Disease constantly waits for the bars of resistance to be dropped in order that it may pounce upon the human body and destroy it.

The government exercises its functions with regard to carbolic acid, strychnine, cocaine, opium, etc., because they are speedy in their action, but certainly the speed of their destructive powers should not determine their use or their sale.

Judge Landis at Freeport, Ill., tried a case of interstate shipment of misbranded goods. The offense had occurred more than a year before and the Judge being "satisfied" that the violation of the law was "not deliberate," imposed a "nominal" fine of "one cent."

. The Solicitor of the Department of Agriculture can possibly tell us why the United States Government, which controls the sale of chloroform and ether, does not control the sale of flavoring extracts made of chloroform and ether.

Perhaps the best legislators and the best public officials are men who are more interested in humanity than in political success. In the meantme the question is: "Are we going to do anything about it?"

The Commissioner at Albany and his New York assistants have accomplished wonderful results, with their limited means, in prosecuting butter frauds and olive oil adulterations. But rotten eggs, dirty milk, villainous compounds that masquerade as jams

and jellies and catsups and fruit syrups, adulterated
spices, coffee coated with lead chromoate and Venetian red, cream thickened with calcium sucrate,
oysters and fish preserved with borax, baker's cakes
colored with "egg color," a coal-tar dye, chocolate
icing colored with another aniline preparation, egg
puffs made with gelatine and saponin, old canned
goods relabeled on the outside and tainted with the
irritant salts of tin on the inside, synthetic flavoring
extracts, pickles and mince meat and chow-chow preserved with alum and many other vicious practices
still flourish because, as a State, New York has not
opened its eyes to the danger.

We cannot inform our readers why the Stilwell
pure food bill of 1911 was "buried in committee"
because we do not know. That question remains
for the Food and Drugs Commission, appointed by
Governor Dix, to answer. In due time we may know
who among New York State's representatives at
Albany are representing the people and who are
representing the food corruptors. In the meantime
we know that one official in a high place openly de-
fended benzoate of soda because when he eats catsup
preserved with that drug he finds that "gases which
have collected in his stomach are released." This
proves to him, as he declares, that benzoate is harmless, and "in conscience he must spread the truth
for the benefit of others similarly afflicted!"

Ice cream has been the subject of some serious
prosecutions by the Government. To interfere with
the adulterators the bad ice cream has had to be
caught on its way from one State into another. The
products so shipped on which prosecution was based
were declared to have "consisted in whole or in part
of a filthy decomposed and putrid animal substance

which renders the articles unfit for food." The Government proved in these cases that as many as 500,000,000 bacteria were found in a cubic centimeter, approximately a half teaspoonful of the ice cream. The bacteria consisted largely of colon bacilli, which abound in human and animal refuse. The evidence showed that the ice cream was manufactured in low, poorly ventilated rooms, that in some places the workmen worked in slimy water, and that at one plant horses were stabled on the same floor on which the ingredients for the ice cream were mixed. The formula for the seized ice cream called for a chemically treated product of renovated butter, skimmed and condensed milk, desiccated or broken and frozen eggs, cornstarch, gelatine, synthetic flavorings and coloring matter.

The St. Louis, Cincinnati and Chicago seizures were particularly filthy, and in their making a machine known as a "homogenizer" was employed. This machine extracts the fat from rancid butter and mixes the material from which the ice cream is made. With the aid of gelatine such a machine will produce a "fluffy" product. There are about sixty commercial formulas used in New York by ice cream makers. The Government cannot touch them. Their adulterations fall under the control of the State Department of Agriculture and the Health Department. The State does not profess to be able to meet the situation and the health authorities are busy with other things.

The extensive use of ice cream by children makes regulation of this product as imperative as the regulation of the milk supply. There is no better culture medium than milk and gelatine for the development of pathogenic bacteria, and the importance of crusading against low grade ice cream is a summer issue. Much of the bowel trouble reported by the local Health Department among children under five years of age may have its origin in infected frozen dainties. There should be no speculation about this matter. What the city demands is safety and certainty.

Dr. Wiley has established standards for ice cream. To what extent are these standards followed in New York City, where, as far as Dr. Wiley is concerned, it is not necessary to follow any standards? Who is safeguarding New York's ice cream supply?

If you suppose that sodium benzoate and sodium sulphite have no effect on digestion, you can perform a simple experiment at home that will change your attitude toward the question of food preservatives.

Sodium benzoate needs no description. Its history has been written in the most shameless phrases ever coined by political and commercial corruption. Few, however, know what it is and how it acts as a preservative of food products. It is prepared by the action of benzoic acid on the metal sodium which yields salt, pure white in color and slightly acrid to the taste.

Sodium sulphite, not so well known and usually employed by the butcher under the name of "preservaline," is prepared by the action of sulphurous acid on the metal sodium. The resultant salt resembles the benzoate salt in color, but has a nauseating taste, and, when placed upon the tongue, produces a strangling sensation in the throat.

Grind one pound of lean beef in a meat chopper. Divide it into three equal parts. Mix with each part about 20 per cent of finely chopped pineapple. The juice of the pineapple is a solvent of flesh and in the quantity mentioned will perfectly digest beef at ordinary atmospheric temperature. Place each of the three parts of chopped beef and pineapple in three separate vessels. Mark No. 1 as the "control" mixture. Set it aside.

Into mixture No. 2 carefully distribute one-half of 1 per cent sodium benzoate. Set it aside.

To mixture No. 3 add in the same intimate manner one-half of one per cent sodium sulphite. Set it aside.

At the end of twenty-four hours the beef in vessel No. 1, containing no preservative, will be mottled brown and gray in color and perfectly digested. The living enzymes of digestion have done their work. In fact, only a pulp will remain. This pulp, digested with pineapple juice, is the predigested meat prepared for the physician's prescription.

The beef in vessel No. 2 will be salmon pink in color. The sodium benzoate has arrested the action of the pineapple juice. It is an enemy of digestion. It suspends the laws of nature. It kills the digestive enzymes. It keeps the tomb sweet. The Egyptians knew this. Their mummies were preserved with benzoic acid.

The beef in vessel No. 3 will be a brilliant red, such as you see in the window of a butcher shop, where a platter of hamburger steak or a string of frankfurters is displayed. Like the benzoate it has prevented digestion. Outside the stomach these drugs, in such common use, have an inhibiting effect on digestion. What is their conduct inside? Why are they used? Why are so many of the people apparently so indifferent to their action?

What is the remedy? Politics? No. Chicanery and abuse of a devoted public servant? No. Enforcement of the law and prison for the offender? Yes.

The custom of "sweating" coffee to give it the appearance of green coffee properly aged is questionable. Green coffee improves with age before it is subjected to the roasting process, on which it depends largely for its agreeable flavor and aroma. It is probably true that there is nothing in the practice of this coffee trick which might be considered deleterious.

But to give inferior grades of coffee a coating of lead chromate is only to deceive the trade into mistaking a poor quality of coffee for a superior one. The practice of painting coffee with Venetian red is a pernicious sham which should be punished by law.

Oil of cinnamon, oil of cloves, oil of mustard, oil of cassia, etc., are extensively employed in the arts. Spices are robbed of their fixed and volatile oils to supply this demand. As a result low grade and exhausted spice, little better than so much wood fibre, is sold to the people. In addition to these spice frauds, "tailing" and "siftings," dirt and waste, are mixed with pepper, cinnamon, cloves, etc., and the public is duped with misleading labels and so-called cheap packages that are practically worthless. The dull gray substance often sold as white pepper is a bleached product worth about one-fourth the price paid for it. True white pepper is creamy white. It is rare.

Olives known to the trade as "culls" and "seconds" are packed in the same bottle with prime fruit, and the bargain finds its way sometimes to the discriminating table.

There is no such thing as "full cream cheese." The best types of cheese sold as cream cheese are made of whole milk artificially colored with coal-tar dye. It is said that people will not eat white cheese, the natural product. Skim milk cheese is the rule. It has been robbed of its valuable butter fats and is not so nutritious or digestible or palatable as whole milk cheese, but it is largely manufactured as a substitute for the honest product. Lard is used as a filler, and barium sulphate, a heavy mineral, is employed to give weight.

Caramels are manufactured from the "swells" of the condensed milk industry. These "swells" are spoiled by the generation of gas-producing bacteria. They are as unfit for food as the tomato pulp, so largely employed in the making of tomato soup, catsup and chili sauce by the unscrupulous manufacturer. The heat to which these bacteria are subjected in the caramel-making kills the bacteria but has no effect on the end-products of the bacteria. Those end-products have no good part to play in the body of a living child.

In certain quarters there has been bitter criticism of those who expose the secrets of the food industry. Such secrets ought not to exist. They have become part of the permanent records of the Department of Agriculture and have found their way into practically all of the annual reports of the various State chemists. That they have not had larger publicity is due to the fact that the "Notices of Judgment" do not usually find their way into newspaper offices.

The attack on Dr. Wiley has stimulated interest in the crimes of the food world, and in many quarters the overzealous food fakers are now looked upon as commercial suicides who by their own folly have hastened the end of their criminal practices.

Special Agent Harry P. Cassidy, of the Pennsylvania State Dairy and Food Department, in the month of August, 1910, began action against a wholesale confectioner of Philadelphia charging him with selling candy containing sulphur dioxide or sulphurous acid. Samples of the wholesaler's candy relishes and other penny specialties had been analyzed by Professor Charles H. LaWall, Chemist for the State Dairy and Food Commission, and were found to contain sulphurous acid.

It must be remembered that all New Orleans molasses contains sulphurous acid and it is impossible to make candy free from sulphurous acid from such molasses.

The case against the wholesaler had hardly got started when the National Candy Manufacturers' Association, represented in almost every large city throughout the United States, obtained a temporary injunction in the United States District Court, restraining Cassidy from going ahead with the prosecution. After two months, the court, refusing a permanent injunction, dissolved its prior order.

Cassidy then brought the candy manufacturer to trial in Common Pleas Court where the jury brought in a verdict of guilty. Judge Martin then upset the verdict and the case was started on its way to the higher courts. Cassidy was being hampered in every way by legal technicalities and delays in establishing the right of the State of Pennsylvania to prohibit the sale of poisoned candy, but he did not falter.

Finally Judge Henderson of the Superior Court, declaring that "no one has a natural or a constitutional right to put poison in confectionery or other foods" imposed a sentence of guilty which was immediately appealed.

The case was then taken to the Supreme Court and in a decision rendered in April, 1912, after almost two years of fighting against the spirit of darkness, the highest court in the State of Pennsylvania upheld the opinion of the Superior Court striking a blow at Pennsylvania candy manufacturers who use sulphurous acid or any other poison in their products.

Unscrupulous candy manufacturers in the State of Pennsylvania cannot now take refuge behind the contention that a law which safeguards the health of the public is unconstitutional when it trespasses against property rights or interferes with business.

Something happens every day to make people realize the gravity of the odds under which they live, but they continue to go along as before, unmindful of the evil things around them which by their united and intelligent action they can destroy.

But in the meantime charges were brought against Cassidy and he was dismissed from the service of the state. The governor of Pennsylvania was brought into the case, gave Cassidy the hearing demanded, was forced to vindicate him, just as Dr. Wiley was vindicated, but Cassidy was not restored to office.

Both Wiley and Cassidy are "out" and now in Pennsylvania, having learned the lesson, no official will dare go after the big cases. Look for loose enforcement of the law in Pennsylvania.

CHAPTER XIV.

A RAID ON IMPURE FOODS.

In the city of Worcester, Mass., on the evening of March 21, 1912, there was a Domestic Science and Pure Food Exposition in Mechanic's Hall, conducted by Retail Grocers' and Provision Dealers' Association and the Worcester Women's Club with a membership of six hundred.

There were forty-six exhibits, many of them giving samples to the visitors, and a laboratory in charge of Lewis B. Allyn, Professor of Chemistry and Physics in the Massachusetts State Normal School.

Three of the young lady students of the Westfield School were demonstrating to the housewives methods by which adulteration can be detected in food products.

Downstairs in Washburn Hall a lecture was given by the writer, telling something of the crimes recorded in this volume. But the audience listened quietly. They do not believe that such things are going on in Worcester.

Little impression was made upon the citizens of Worcester. But the next morning, March 22nd, two men planned an excursion through the drug stores, bake shops and grocery shops of the city.

Easter confectionery is purchased consisting of candy eggs, licorice pellets, "baked beans," Easter rabbits, Easter chicks, candy marbles, chocolate creams, fourteen different varieties of sweet meats.

Strawberry soda water, orangeade, lime juice and Sauterne wine are purchased.

Next, chili sauce, sour pickles, canned mushrooms, dried apples, dried apricots, onion salad, lemon pie, mince pie, raspberry turnovers, egg puffs, orange cake, lemon extract, vanilla extract, prepared mustard, brussels sprouts, maraschino cherries are added to the list.

Cough syrups, consumption cures, seven different soothing syrups and teething syrups, kidney pills, headache cures are bought. They are all taken to the laboratory and analyzed.

The Easter eggs are made of stearic acid, carpenter's glue, glucose, coal-tar dye and soap-stone.

The licorice pellets are made of lamp black, carpenter's glue and glucose.

The "baked beans" are coated with shellac.

The Easter rabbits and marshmallows are made of carpenter's glue, glucose, coal-tar dyes and ethereal flavors.

The Easter chicks are made of carpenter's glue, glucose, coal-tar dyes and ethereal flavorings.

The candy marbles are made of coal-tar dye, glucose, ethereal flavoring and soap stone.

One-half of one of the little yellow chicks purchased for a penny gives up enough carpenter's glue to bind two boards five inches wide and nine inches long together.

The lime juice contains sulphurous acid.

The canned mushrooms contain sulphurous acid.

The dried apples and dried apricots contain sulphurous acid.

The Sauterne wine contains sulphurous acid.

The strawberry soda water contains coal-tar dye, benzoate of soda and ethereal flavor.

The orangeade contains coal-tar dye.

One of the thirst quenchers contains caffeine.

The onion salad contains one-tenth of one per cent benzoate of soda, two-tenths of one per cent aluminum sulphate and one-tenth of one per cent saccharin. Food drugs get lonely sometimes and travel in battalions.

The maraschino cherries are bleached with sulphurous acid, dyed with analine and preserved with benezoate of soda.

The sour pickles contain aluminum sulphate.

The lemon pie contains glycerine, glucose, oil of lemon, starch, coal-tar dye and benzoate of soda. The pie filler from which it is made came to the baker in a barrel. The barrel is properly labeled. The pie is not labeled. The mince pie contains benzoate of soda. The mince meat from which it is made is properly labeled. The pie is not labeled. The raspberry turnovers contain coal-tar dye and benzoate of soda.

The cough syrup is labeled "contains no chloroform, ether or morphine—a purely vegetable compound." At the bottom of the label appear the words: "Alcohol 2½%, Tincture of Poppy 2⅛." That cough syrup says nothing about laudanum. The innocent phrase "vegetable" or "purely vegetable" means nothing. Strychnine, morphine, laudanum are "purely vegetable."

The soothing syrups and teething syrups are found to contain morphine, morphine sulphate, morphine hydrochloride, chloral hydrate, cannabis indica and chloroform.

The consumption cure is found to contain alcohol and chloroform; headache cures contain acetanilid, antipyrin, acetphenetidin; the kidney pills contain an illegal coal-tar dye, methylene blue so concentrated that one pill gives a blue tint to one hundred gallons of water.

These damnable things are going to go!!!

The lemon extract is found to be misbranded, sold under the name of a chemical laboratory that has no existence. The vanilla extract is a compound made of vanillin and coumarin, not of vanilla beans.

The molasses contains sulphur dioxide, and the brussels sprouts, sulphate of copper.

Another day a big bake shop is visited. Its manager has read the report of the lecture of the night before in the "Morning Telegram." He is panic-stricken and does not refuse an inspection of his plant. The tubs and barrels in the rear are plainly marked "artificially colored, artificially flavored, preserved with benzoate, etc." He promises that these supplies will be thrown out of his shop.

Another bake shop is visited; in the rear room where the baking is done dirty workers are seen. A copper kettle is boiling over a coal fire. In the kettle is a sugar sauce. Flecks of dirt are being skimmed from the surface of the mass. The ashes raked out on the floor are piled high around the stove. A coating of grease and filth is found on the woodwork of the room to the depth of one-eighth of an inch. Artificial colors, egg powders, compounds, dyes, fillers, etc., abound.

The Worcester "Evening Gazette" carries two columns reporting the exposures. The Saturday "Morning Telegram" on its front page carries a three column head line.

The members of the Worcester Woman's Club and their aroused friends met in Washburn Hall Saturday night, March 24th and present for open discussion resolutions calling upon President Taft to reinstate Doctor Wiley.

The resentment of the city as expressed through its organized womanhood is white hot. Every man and woman present, with the exception of one, endorses the resolution. One man rises to his feet and protests. He is a wealthy citizen of Worcester, the proprietor of a patent medicine. After the meeting he comes upstairs to the laboratory followed by the crowd. He is challenged in the open and asked to explain why he voted against Dr. Wiley. He is informed that the borax industry, the blended whiskey industry, the dried fruit industry, the drugged pickle industry, the rice industry, the white flour industry, the molasses industry, the preserving industry, the mince meat industry, the manufacturers of saccharin and its users, the manufacturers of sulphites and the users of this drug, the manufacturers of food dyes and their users, the manufacturers of alum and its users, the manufacturers of bleached glucose and the leather industries that use glucose as a filler, the importers of opium, morphine, cocaine and their users, the users of nostrums, containing habit-forming drugs, the patent medicine industry, the benzoate of soda industry are against Doctor Wiley, against uncompromised purity of food products, against food reform.

He is informed that 150,000 ounces of cocaine are used in patent medicines in the United States every year; that large quantities of acetanilid, acetphenetidin, antipyrin, phenacetin, caffeine, chloral hydrate, codein, dionin, heroin are consumed annually; that tons of opium are used every year in preparing patent medicines; that there are more than a hundred sanitariums in the United States advertising treatment for drug-addiction; that many hundreds of cases of drug addiction are treated annually by physicians in private practice and in hospitals; that there are more than thirty so-called mail order drug addiction cures on the market and that the manager of one of these treatments has openly confessed that his company has 100,000 names of drug-addicts upon its books.

He is informed that in the year 1910 in the United States infants under one year of age to the number of 154,373 died; that the total number of deaths of children under ten years of age in the same year was 235,262; that in the year 1910 there were officially recorded at Washington, D. C., a total of 804,512 deaths.

He is informed that Doctor Wiley never claimed that he did not make mistakes, but that where there was a question of corporate interests on one hand and human health on the other, Doctor Wiley's attitude was always uncompromising, and that, therefore, Doctor Wiley made enemies; that the things then discovered in Worcester are the things against which Wiley has been devoting twenty-nine years of his active life.

He is informed that the Bureau of Chemistry with Doctor Wiley at its head spent $1,190,784 in preparing evidence against food frauds, not one of which frauds was permitted by Dr. Wiley's superiors to be reported to the Federal courts for prosecution, and that it cost the government $515 to gather evidence in the Bureau of Chemistry for every one of the 6,206 suppressed cases that were kept out of the hands of the public prosecutor through influence higher-up.

He is told that Doctor Wiley was accused of crimes by his associates in office and that the Attorney General of the United States recommended that "condign punishment" should be visited upon him, and that an investigation compelled President

Taft, in spite of the Doctor's enemies, to vindicate him sweepingly.

He is informed that Doctor Wiley's misdeeds, so deserving of "condign punishment" were not misdeeds at all, were laudable efforts to preserve the health of the people against the food and drug crimes which are committed in all places just as in the city of Worcester.

A child's Easter hat is held up, brilliantly trimmed. The straw was bleached with sulphurous acid. The scarlet ribbon bows were colored with the coaltar dye extracted from the strawberry soda; the blue rosette received its happy hue from the coaltar dye extracted from a kidney pill; the lavender buds were colored with coal-tar dye extracted from the Easter confectionery, and the Maraschino cherries which added a delightful touch of brilliant color to this piece of millinery perfection, contained three drugs, sulphur dioxide, analine and benzoate. It was a pure food hat!

A breathless crowd surrounds Doctor Garst to listen to his answer. In a trembling voice he speaks to the crowd. "I admit Doctor Wiley has done a great, good work and is deserving of all honor. I am in sympathy with everythng that has been revealed here to-night and I have stood in this room for an hour listening to the exposures that have been made. I admire Doctor Wiley because he has been fighting these things and the reason I voted against him downstairs is because there was nobody present to defend the doctor's enemies."

Worcester is awake at last. Is it to be alone?

CHAPTER XV.

FOOD ADULTERATIONS.

To show that these conditions exist generally, we quote from a report by John Phillips Street, Chemist of the Connecticut Agricultural Experiment Station, of the results secured in his laboratory during the past four years. All food examinations under the law in Connecticut are made in Mr. Street's laboratory at the State Experiment Station. The station, however, has no power to prosecute and only reports its findings to the proper officials and then, if prosecution follows, furnishes expert testimony in court.

In Interstate cases when the dealer produces a properly signed guaranty the case is taken out of the hands of the state official and turned over to the Department at Washington. That department suppressed many thousand cases that were never again heard of by the public. "Business," not the health of the people, was the motive.

Mr. Street says: "The following summary shows the results of our examinations in Connecticut in the past four years, remembering that these figures apply to foods only, not drugs, and that under the heading, "adulterated" are included misbranding, below standard and other violations of the law.

Year.	Not found Adulterated.	Adulterated.	Compound.	Total.
1908	639	228	100	967
1909	682	262	85	1,029
1910	641	262	54	959
1911	389	479	70	938
Total	2,351	1,233	309	3,893

"The above tabulation does not include 24 samples of infant and invalid foods, 37 of ice cream and 11 of canned peas, for which we have no standards in this state. The amount of adulteration in the peas was very high, 56 containing glucose, 77 cane sugar, 14 copper, 88 tin, and 16 "soaked" peas. The table shows that during the four years 3,893 samples of food were examined, only 60.4 per cent of which were pure. The 51 samples of sausage and the 452 of molasses included in the above were not examined for chemical preservatives. Such an examination would doubtless have still further reduced the purity percentage.

"The following tabulation gives in detail our findings with the different classes of foods examined during the four years:

	Not found Adulterated.	Adulterated.	Compound.
Breakfast Foods............	36	14	..
Butter	86	172	24
Cider	2	4	*
Chocolate and Cocoa........	43	45	23
Coffee	29	1	..
Condensed Milk	33	4	..
Cream	49	6	6
Cream of Tartar...........	4	..	..
Dessert Preparations.......	2	1	14

	Not found Adulterated.	Adulter- ated.	Com- pound.
Diabetic Foods	11	10	..
Flavoring Extracts	132	161	61
Fruit Colors and Flavors	8	3	1
Fruit Juices	19	9	17
Gelatin	10	6	..
Ice Cream Cones	22	6	..
Ice Cream Powders	1	..	..
Jams, Jellies and Preserves	14	8	67
Ketchup	5	54	19
Lard	97	12	..
Maple Syrup	8	..	23
Meat Extracts and Juices	13	39	..
Milk	295	346	..
Mince Meat	17	1	1
*Molasses	452	2	..
Olive Oil	125	10	..
Paprika	12	2	1
Pickles	15	5	15
Relishes	2	2	8
Salad Dressings	9	1	2
Root Beer Extracts	11	1	..
Salt	18	..	3
Sardines	43	1	..
Sauces	23	5	3
†Sausage	26	25	..
Soda Water and Soda Water Syrups	6	42	2
Soft Drinks	7	2	..
Soups	21	..	..
Starches	29	..	..
Spices	82	13	..
Vinegar	534	220	14
Total	2,351	1,233	309
Percentage	60.4	31.7	7.9

*Examined only for glucose.
†Examined only for starch.

"I have classified the different kinds of adulteration detected in my work in this state during the past four years. Many of these are of course harmless adulterants. This list includes only actual adulterants and does not cover misbranded or substandard samples, nor does it include skimmed milk, watered milk, dilute alcohol and deficient oil in flavoring extracts, sulphites in sausage and molasses, or any vinegar adulterants.

"The following non-chemical adulterants were found the number of times indicated: 40 apple stock, 1 living beetle, 11 beef stearin, 1 Bombay mace, 1 brown sugar, 126 cane sugar, 3 capsicum, 54 caramel, 1 cayenne, 2 coffee hulls, 2 corn starch, 13 cotton seed oil, 1 exhausted ginger, 117 glucose, 1 honey, 1 molasses, 178 oleomargarine or renovated butter, 3 olive oil, 1 olive stones, 1 rice product, 4 sand, 16 soaked peas, 45 starch, 19 tumeric and 2 wheat products, or 644 in all.

The following chemicals were found the times stated:

Alcohol 13
Alum 39
Benzoic Acid 173
Boric Acid 4
Caffeine 1
Calcium carbonate 1
Calcium phosphate 1
Calcium sulphate 1
Coumarin 40
Coal-tar colors 189
Copper sulphate 14
Formaldehyde 5
Glycerine 5
Hydrocyanic acid 2
Magnesium carbonate 1

Nitrobenzol 1
Phosphoric acid 1
Potassium nitrate 11
Saccharin 38
Salicylic acid............................ 6
Sodium phosphate 1
Sucrate of lime 8
Sulphurous acid 5
Synthetic flavors 67
Tartaric acid 3
Tin 89
Wood alcohol 2

Total 721

"Certainly the above figures do not indicate that
chemicals are of rare occurrence in foods. Twenty-
seven different chemicals were found 721 times in
about 3,900 samples of food. It is also of interest
to note the distribution of these chemicals among
the different kinds of foods. Alcohol was found in
soft drinks, fruit syrups, cider and meat extracts;
alum in pickles and relishes; benzoic acid in jams,
jellies, preserves, chili sauce, pickles, soft drinks,
catsup, mince meat, fruit syrups, lime juice, orangeade, lemon juice, root beer extracts, relishes and
soda water; boric acid in ice cream cones and salad
dressing; caffeine in soft drinks; calcium carbonate,
phosphate and sulphate in salt; coal-tar colors in
jams, jellies, preserves, jelly powders, lemon, pepper-
mint, orange, pineapple, raspberry, strawberry and
wintergreen extracts, catsup, orangeade, fruit
syrups, ice cream cones, ice cream powders, salad
dressings and soda water; copper sulphate in canned
peas; coumarin in vanilla extract; formaldehyde in
milk; glycerine in flavoring extracts; hydrocyanic

acid in almond extract; magnesium carbonate in salt; nitrobenzol in almond extract; phosphoric acid in jams; potassum nitrate in meat extracts; saccharin in jams, jellies, pickles, soft drinks, catsup, relishes, Worcestershire sauce and soda water; salicylic acid in meat extracts and strawberry syrup; sodium phosphate in salt; sulphurous acid in mince meat and lime juice; sucrate of lime in cream; synthetic flavors in jelly powders; flavoring extracts, ice cream powders and soda water; tartaric acid in jams and jellies; tin in preserves and canned peas; wood alcohol in lemon extract."

If one state in this Union can present the above unfortunate array of facts, what might not all the States show?"

But there are still other ways to rob foods of the value which nature intended they should possess.

Nowhere is man's foolish interference with nature more evident than in his thoughtless destruction of one of nature's oldest gifts to the human race—the olive.

We do not pluck the unripe grape, the green peach, the green strawberry or any other green fruit and then "cure" it by chemical treatment in order to destroy the ferments with which nature endowed it, thereby preventing the glorious transformation which the processes of ripening bring about according to nature's fixed law to every immature thing of earth.

But man arrests the development of the olive, stunts its beauty and destroys its virtue. The beautiful purple fruit of the southern hills is not permitted to ripen as nature would have it do. It is plucked green and tossed to chemistry to be made a curse to the race it was destined to serve.

To-day the ripe olive is despised and in its luscious, nutritious stead, the crisp, green thing of an evil art rolls across the Atlantic in thousands of puncheons to add its part to the tragedy of food.

Man converts thousands of acres of golden corn into glucose, using in the manufacture hydrochloric acid to produce the syrup desired.

Man converts thousands of acres of barley and rice into beer and millions of pounds of grapes into fermented wine. The natural sugar of the fruit and its precious mineral salts are destroyed by the process. In their helpful stead, man substitutes thousands of gallons of alcohol, the initial cost of which is but a few cents per gallon, but with revenue tax, transportation charges, rectifiers' and blenders' profit, bonded warehouse charge, liquor dealers' profit, advertising expense, this alcohol reaches him at a cost from $4.00 to $8.00 per gallon.

No, we cannot attempt here to cover the entire field of food adulteration and debasement. This effort to prove that food and food preparation are the most important stones in the foundation of a strong and enduring nation, will rest when it has aroused the boards of trade, health departments and legislators all over the country.

To show the manner in which the benzoate of soda users misuse the law's permission to employ this chemical in their food products, the following cases are quoted from the report of the State Chemist, Department of Agriculture, Georgia, issued September, 1912:

"Squire-Dingee Company, Chicago, Ill."

Catsup—Labelled to contain ".1 of 1% benzoate of soda," was found to contain .30 of 1% benzoate of soda and declared "illegal."

"S. J. Van Hill Company, Baltimore, Md."

Catsup—Labelled to contain ".1 of 1% benzoate of soda," was found to contain .36%, nearly four times as much as declared. "Illegal."

"Gast, Crofts and Company, Louisville, Ky."

Catsup—Labelled to contain ".1 of 1% benzoate of soda," was found to contain .39%. "Illegal."

"Kentucky Canning Company, Owensboro, Ky."

Catsup—Labelled to contain ".1 of 1% benzoate of soda," was found to contain .38%. "Illegal."

"Jobber-Bishop & Company, New York."

Catsup—Labelled to contain ".1% benzoate of soda," was found to contain .2%. "Illegal."

"Jones Brothers & Company, Lousville , Ky."

Catsup—Labelled to contain ".1% benzoate of soda," was found to contain .35%. "Illegal."

"Beach Lake Canning Company, Cuthbert, Ga."

Catsup—Labelled to contain ".1% benzoate of soda," was found to contain .28%. "Illegal."

"Knadler & Lucas, Louisville, Ky."

Catsup—Labelled to contain ".1% benzoate of soda," was found to contain .22%. "Illegal."

"Hort-Catto Manufacturing Co., Detroit, Mich."

Catsup—Labelled to contain ".1% benzoate of soda," was found to contain .28%. "Illegal."

"J. Weller Company, Cincinnati, Ohio."

Catsup—Labelled to contain ".1% benzoate of soda," was found to contain .22% benzoate of soda. "Illegal."

"Curtiss Brothers Company, Rochester, N. Y."

Blue Label Catsup—Was declared illegal, because it was found to contain .2% benzoate of soda.

"Libbey-McNeil & Libby."

Catsup—Was found illegal, because it contained .26% benzoate of soda.

"Charles L. Hersch & Co., New York."

Catsup—Labelled to contain ".1% benzoate of soda," was found to contain .40% benzoate of soda. "Illegal."

"Williams Brothers Company, Detroit, Mich."

Catsup—Labelled to contain ".1% benzoate of soda," was found to contain .22%. "Illegal."

"E. G. Daily & Company, Detroit, Mich."

Catsup—Labelled to contain ".1% benzoate of soda," was found to contain .40%. "Illegal."

These official findings indicate that the food manufacturer, who avails himself of the law's permission to use one-tenth of 1% benzoate of soda, or any other per cent, provided he truthfully declares the per cent on the label of his product, only too frequently disregards the law, and uses benzoate of soda in quantities ranging from twice to four times as much as the label indicates.

The above facts are taken from serial No. 56, compiled by J. J. Conner, Commissioner of Agriculture of the State of Georgia.

CHAPTER XVI.

All the Sauterne wines and sweet white wine, all New Orleans and Porto Rico molasses, all artificial Sultana raisins, all California "silver" prunes, all California dried apricots, dried peaches and dried pears, all dried apples with the exception of sun-dried apples plainly marked as such, most canned mushrooms and considerable canned asparagus are bleached and preserved with sulphurous acid. Other foods such as Maraschino cherries, gelatine, jelly powders and "export" glucose also contain sulphurous acid.

On July 13th, 1907, five years ago, the authorities at Washington declared that pending investigation of the effect of sulphurous acid upon the health of the people, the Department of Agriculture would institute no action against the manufacturers of foods and drinks who employed sulphurous acid as a bleaching agent and preservative.

Sulphurous acid is still legal and is being consumed in hundreds of tons of foods and drinks representing the industries of many states.

On October 2nd, 1911, Doctor J. C. Olsen, Professor of Chemistry of the Polytechnic Institute, Brooklyn, said at Madison Square Garden, New York City, that he had introduced sulphurous acid into the food of dogs and watched them closely for six months. At first they actually appeared to fatten on it and it was thought that all the cry against sul-

phurous acid would be proved to be without foundation.

Then the animals were chloroformed and cut
open. Apparently all their organs were sound and
healthy and as far as the naked eye was concerned
sulphurous acid had not harmed them. Before a
jury with only such surface evidence sulphurous acid
would be white-washed and the experiments on dogs
would be considered conclusive.

But Dr. Olsen was thorough. He placed the
dogs' kidneys under the microscope. In every instance the results were the same. The lens revealed
the degeneration of the kidney cells. They had
broken down. Sulphurous acid was found to be
deadly to the kidneys of dogs.

Scientists do not yet know to what extent sulphurous acid combines with the organic minerals of
the fruits of which it becomes artificially a part, or
how far it changes the nature of the mineral salts.

Yet they find that it produces injurious effects on
the human organs.

Dr. Wiley, after his clinical experiments in the
Bureau of Chemistry, denounced the use of sulphurous acid as an ingredient of foods and proved by
medical and pathological data that it produces
serious injury to digestion and health. His findings
were reported in Circular No. 37 issued by the Department of Agriculture, November 22nd, 1907.
That circular stated plainly:

"The administration of sulphurous acid in
the food produces serious disturbances of the
metabolic functions. It adds an immense burden to the kidneys which cannot result in
anything but injury. It impoverishes the blood
in respect to the number of red and white cor-

puscles therein, and the administration of a substance which diminishes these important component particles of the blood is in every sense highly prejudicial to health."

The fruit growers of California demand its use. Under its action dried fruit takes up as much as twelve or fifteen per cent of moisture and this moisture is sold to the fruit packers at fruit prices. The fruit packers then redip the fruit in a solution of hot glucose and water, thereby adding more weight or filler to their products. This necessitates another treatment with sulphurous acid in order to make the fruit marketable. So the people pay for moisture when they buy fruit! And glucose as a filler finds its way into a hundred foods.

This is why there is opposition between the national health on one hand and the fruit, molasses and wine interests on the other, and hence, government reluctance to decide between them.

It is possible to obtain unbleached molasses. The molasses known as "Barbadoes" is free from sulphurous acid.

It is possible to obtain sun-dried fruits. Demand them.

Your demand will accomplish quickly what the law for five years has not accomplished.

In the meantime no one may say to what degree sulphurous acid has contributed its part to the making of those mortality records at Washington which include Death's annual harvest of 235,262 children.

Five years ago, July 13, 1907, Doctor Frederick L. Dunlap and Solicitor George P. McCabe declared in Food Inspection Decision No. 76:

"It is the opinion of the Board that copper sulphate is injurious and should be prohibited eventually, but it would work a great injury to American importers to put this ruling into effect at once. It is believed that the use of copper sulphate or of other salts of copper in restricted quantities for greening vegetables should be permitted for the pack of the present year, but for no longer."

Five years have past and sulphate of copper remains one of the food drugs which are legal. As in the decision which permitted the use of sulphurous acid, Dr. Wiley in this case did not sign the circular permitting manufacturers to use the drug.

In three states—North Carolina, Pennsylvania and Texas—the health authorities have condemned copper salts as an ingredient of canned fruits and vegetables, and those States have responded by enacting laws that forbid the sale of any article of food contaminated with copper.

Does the housewife know that nearly all the string beans, lima beans, brussels sprouts and peas imported into the United States from France are artificially colored—discolored is the correct word—with sulphate of copper? The American canner does not use this drug at all and to this extent deserves great praise. It is a curious situation. The Federal pure food laws permit the importation of coppered canned goods, though Pennsylvania, North Carolina and Texas declare that copper salts are poisonous and refuse to permit any traffic in them in those States, under penalty of the law.

The French themselves will not eat the canned vegetables which they treat with copper for our use. The dealers plead that the public demands food made attractive by chemical manipulation. So the manufacturers make their strongest appeal to the eye. Next they consider the sense of smell, then the sense of taste, and last the question of nutritive value. The folly of this practice is obvious.

The public wants what looks like the greatest and most attractive value for its money. In reality that value is nutritive value.

Coloring by copper salts is a fraud. It deceives the consumer by influencing him to mistake an artificial and dangerous characteristic as an indication of superior merit. In the "Revue Scientifique," Klopine reports that certain cells of the human organism have a selective action on green, and that this coloring substance is absorbed by the cells until they break down and die. This process goes on continually when an individual habitually uses food that has been artificially colored.

In New York the admirable Stilwell bill, in the nineteen hundred and eleven session at Albany, provided for the banishment of copper salts and all other forms of chemical treatment, but the bill was killed as the "food industries" must not suffer through such a trifling issue as "pure food!"

If in the opinion of the Board of Food and Drug Inspection, sulphate of copper is injurious and should be prohibited eventually, why should the Board of Food and Drugs Inspection add that to prohibit it at once would work a great injury to American importers?

Is the business of American importers of more moment than the health of the American people?

[Editor's Note: Since the above was written a decision has appeared forbidding the importation after Jan. 1, 1913, of any foods containing this poison, but it does not forbid the sale of the $1,000,-000 worth of these coppered foods which New York importers got into the country during the last three months of 1912.]

Alum is an astringent. It hardens vegetable and animal tissue. Pickles so soft that they can be squeezed through the hand like tooth paste from its tube can be made by alum's use firm enough to sell. Piccalilli, chow-chow, condiments, baking powder, baker's "compounds," mince meat, etc., are put into a "healthy" condition by allopathic doses of alum.

Like all preservatives and drugs of its kind it destroys ferments. We have seen how digestion depends upon the activity of ferments. We can easily understand that alum and other food drugs do not assist these ferments to perform their duties. Is alum's effect upon the mucous membrane of the intestines anything like its effect upon the membrane of the pickle?

Fruits and berries delayed on the railroad, softened and discolored by decay, are not "waste-products" in the estimation of the unscrupulous jam and jelly maker. With the aid of glucose and benzoate of soda they make a compound which juvenile taste persists in demanding through its inheritance of the traditions of grandmother's jam closet.

Such a compound is a dark, syrupy substance, unsightly and uninviting. A legal coal-tar dye can give it the brightness necessary to catch the eye. It pays a handsome profit to the man who makes it and to the grocer who sells it, but it also discourages the honest product on which the profit is smaller.

Apart from all considerations of health, the tendency of the time is thus hurried toward substitution and fraud. Artificial color and benzoate of soda are symbols of this degradation.

Cheap tomato catsup and chili sauce also explain the food manufacturer's cherished regard for benzoate. Many of these catsups are made from tomato pulp which the government has repeatedly condemned because it is found to contain millions of bacteria to the cubic centimeter. Ninety million such bacteria have been found in a half teaspoonful.

Tomato pulp is a waste product prepared from the skins and cores and sweepings of the canning factory. In its partly decomposed state it is scraped from the floor and put into kegs with the food manufacturer's pet antiseptic. It then goes into storage to be called upon as needed in the making of our cheap condiments. The government characterizes such tomato pulp as consisting in whole or in part of a filthy and decomposed vegetable substance. It is made fit for food by the introduction of the sacred one-tenth of one per cent of benzoate of soda.

We need not consider the harmfulness of benzoate. We might admit that it is harmless, although the experiments which Floyd W. Robison, Chief Chemist of the State of Michigan performed on kittens with benzoate revealed the fact that kittens that got benzoate in their milk, died. Robison as a result of his findings against benzoate was dimissed from the government service by Secretary Wilson "for the good of the service." There was no other cause, no charge against him.

Dr. Daniel R. Lucas has prepared a remarkable paper on benzoate. He shows under what conditions it does become a poison.

Anyway benzoate has a bad history; it encourages fraud; it justifies cheapness rather than honesty.

The housewife should read the label on her can or package and then examine the quality of the product. The absence of fine print on the label may be an indication that the food is "pure," but is no indication that it is of good quality.

For instance, in the case of canned California fruits, the purity of the fruit is probably unquestionable, but in some quarters in the trade seven different grades are recognized and in other quarters nine different grades are found.

The grade may be "double extra," "extra," "extra standard," "standard," "fancy seconds," "seconds," "culls," "watered" or "pie fruit." Each grade is a step downward, but the lowest and most miserable product is just as "pure" as the finest.

It is the same way with corn, tomatoes, peas, etc. The latter may be anything from the finest "Early June Sifted" to "soaked" peas which are simply dried peas soaked soft and canned so that the canner may have the pleasure of selling the ignorant housewife a metal can containing dried peas and water.

The question of "quality" is introduced merely to illustrate the necessity of scrutinizing the characteristics of our food with as much interest as we inspect the reflection of our faces in the looking glass. What we see there, in the purely physical matter of healthy charm, is a result of the food we eat. Let us not fret over the signs of decay if we are unwilling to trace that decay to its source in our food supply.

Listen to these phrases on a label on a can in the butcher shop:

"The ideal preservative for chopped meat, hamburger steak, ribs; loins, cuts of meat, quarters of beef, veal, mutton, poultry and pork sausage."

"In use since eighteen hundred eighty-seven."

"For curing, corning and pickling; for bolognas, frankfurters, etc."

"Sprinkle the preservative over the meat before or while being chopped."

These are among the phrases with which the can of "Preservaline" is labeled. The lid of the can is perforated like a salt shaker. You will find it under the counter of many a butcher shop. The butcher who uses it will admit without compunction that the "dose of sulphites" is used extensively by handlers of meat and meat products.

The rich red color which the white powder imparts to meat is "the most profitable service ever offered to the meat trade." The label declares that it is "used everywhere by the progressive butcher" and is "absolutely indispensable to the sausage maker."

The factory in Brooklyn that manufactures this stuff is a big factory and it turns out enormous quantities every day. Where does it go?

The other word for "preservaline" is sulphites. As much as you can lift on the tip of a pen knife will cause you to strangle if placed on the tongue. It is found in marshmallows as well as in sausage and hamburger steaks, for, while it makes hamburger steaks red, it makes marshmallows white.

Scientists employed by food industries say that it may form a relatively harmless compound with the sugars, proteins and cellulose which are present in food.

The government, in Food Inspection Decision Seventy-Six, stated: "Probably all of these 'combined' forms are not equally inert from a physiological point of view," and in the next paragraph the government adds: "but it is necessary to limit its presence in such cases so as to avoid the presence of excessive quantities of free sulphurous acid, the poisonous effect of which is marked."

In the same Food Inspection Decision, Number Seventy-Six, the government said: "However, the pack of nineteen hundred and seven is now under way, some of it is complete, and sodium benzoate has been used extensively. By another year the manufacturers of these food products will have had ample time to adjust manufacturing conditions in such a manner that the use of sodium benzoate will be unnecessary. The prohibition of the use of sodium benzoate at this time would, it is thought, work a hardship upon the manufacturers of food products out of all proportion to the benefit which would be derived by the people. The use of sodium benzoate for the time being in limited quantities, which are to be plainly stated upon the label, seems to be a fair solution both for the people and for the manufacturer."

The government used the words "by another year" and also "for the time," but five years have passed and benzoate is still used. And so the people of the country continue to enjoy the blessing of these added "harmless" ingredients in their food.

On the thirteenth of July, nineteen hundred and seven, the government issued in Section V of Food Inspection Decision Seventy-Six a list of dyes permitted "pending further investigation."

"Pending further investigation" sounds well and hopeful but the list of dyes, the use of which is granted in foods and foodstuffs "pending further investigation" is to-day as it was then.

RED SHADES:
    107 Amranth.
    56 Ponceau 3R.
    517 Erythrosin.
ORANGE SHADES:
    85 Orange 1.
YELLOW SHADES:
    4 Naphthol Yellow S.

GREEN SHADES:/
   435 Light Green S. F. Yellowish.
BLUE SHADES:
   692 Indigo Disulfoacid.

The decision further states that these coal-tar dyes must be made specifically for use in foods, and must bear a guarantee from the manufacturer that they are free from arsenic and that they represent the actual coal-tar compound whose name they bear.

The dye may be the same dye used in coloring feathers, wearing apparel, tapestry, rugs, etc., but when used for cakes, ice cream, candy, etc., it must be made "specifically for use in cakes, ice cream, candy, etc." and not for rugs or ribbons.

Crown Glossine, with chocolate flavor and harmless color was found by the Bureau of Chemistry to contain arsenic. It is used by the candy maker and its final resting place is the stomach of the child.

- In a Circuit Court of the United States for the Southern District of New York, upon a plea of guilty, the manufacturers of Crown Glossine were fined two hundred dollars.

"Specially Denatured Grain Alcohol Brown Glaze" is a confectioner's shellac employed in the manufacture of penny candies. Because it contained the poisonous wood alcohol which causes blindness or death, the courts imposed upon its makers a fine of fifty dollars and costs.

These two cases are recorded under Notices of Judgment, Number Nine Hundred Sixty-Four and Nine Hundred Seventy-two issued at Washington, D. C., July fifteenth, nineteen hundred and eleven.

When greed impels a criminal to kill and rob his victim the crime is picturesque, and punishment is usually commensurate with the excitement which such a crime inspires. When greed impels a food maker to trifle with poisons and preservatives and dyes, and to disregard the laws of life and death in his reach for profit, the picturesque element is not present. The crime is slow in action. The common food does not affright the soul or fill the mind with dread. Debased foods, particularly ice creams, soft drinks, cakes and candy, belong largely to the children's world—and parents think that children are prone to bowel disorders anyhow.

The sick child suggests no mystery; its upset stomach is to be expected. The illness is taken as a matter of course. Hence, the necessity of caution is not even suggested. Though a particularly heinous food-crime is committed its story rarely gets out of the court room.

There, fifty dollars settles the affair!

There are now about Two Thousand Notices of Judgment, but they have not been read by the people.

The instances just quoted are but a few out of hundreds.

Many persons do not realize that the "condign punishment" intrigue against Wiley was a blow aimed at pure food and drugs, aimed at the home, aimed at the health and happiness of the people.

CHAPTER XVII.

BACTERIA IN FOOD.

Metchnikoff complained that we know really little about death and that, although death has a preponderating place in religions, philosophy, literature and folklore, scientific works pay little attention to it.

When Tolstoi approached the problem and searched for some solution in the writings of scientific men, he found the explanations so trivial and inexact that he grew impatient, then enraged.

Metchnikoff himself did not say that he had found the secret of life or death. He did arouse scientific men. We now realize that in the brilliant achievement of scientists one tremendous field has been unexplored.

Biologists have learned much with and without the microscope. Astronomers have traced the heavens with the telescope and now at Cambridge, Harvard astronomers have completed a photographic map of the entire sky showing about 1,500,000 stars.

Chemists have learned much with the test-tube. We have many volumes on radio-activity, X-Rays, violet rays and the scalpel. We have entire libraries devoted to therapeutics. We have probed deep into the secrets of nature, yet, our scientific men have not taught the plain people how to eat and live.

A plant should apparently die when all its organic forces have been exhausted. In some plants parts of the plant, such as the flowers, die periodically, although the plant itself is not exhausted.

Little Helen's father noticed that among the geraniums which the child had planted some of the flowers were withering while others were still blooming. The death of those withered flowers could not be attributed to the exhaustion of the plant when that plant continued to produce new flowers, even while the old ones were dying.

Metchnikoff, studying these geraniums, threw a wonderful light on the ferments and bacteria that abound in life, vegetable or animal, and revealed certain specific truths that now interest us in the loss of good ferments and in the development of bad ferments.

Bad bacteria in milk and milk products, in eggs and eggs products, in such things as "rots and spots" which have received a clean bill of health under the "expert" testimony of scientists before the courts and which the wholesale baker's supply houses can, therefore, continue to sell to the producer of sponge cake, pound cake, vanilla wafers, ice cream, etc., are not to be ignored.

Bacteria of the bad kind in tomato pulp, catsup, chili sauce, fruit products, milk products and gelatine products have no good work to perform.

Fifty years ago it was not known that all fermentation was due to the action of microscopic plants.

It had been discovered that under certain conditions fermentation ceased much more quickly than under others. In transforming sugar to lactic acid it was found that it was useful to add chalk; otherwise fermentation stopped before the greater part of the sugar had been acted upon.

Then in 1857 Pasteur discovered the lactic acid ferment or bacteria. Pasteur showed that that little micro-organism which can produce lactic acid was killed by the very acid it produced.

In order to help it to live and carry on its work it was necessary to neutralize the excess acid which it produced by adding calcium carbonate to the solution in which it was growing.

After the lactic bacteria produce a certain quantity of lactic acid, they are automatically killed by their own activities. The end-product of fire is ash. In many instances the end-product of bacteria is poison. The bacteria are red lights, not always dangerous in themselves, but by their presence they reveal the presence of other things that are dangerous.

In milk the lactic acid bacteria are killed by auto-intoxication. They poison themselves by their own activity. We know that in milk the death of the bacteria takes place at a time when the milk still contains enough sugar for the nutrition of the bacteria, and, therefore, we know that the bacteria do not die as the result of exhaustion or as the result of a lack of food.

We also know that other bacteria act in the same way. The bacteria that produce butyric acid are also destroyed by the acid they produce.

Yeast bacteria which produce alcohol are destroyed by the alcohol they produce, and as soon as a certain limit of alcoholic strength has been reached the yeast dies. When the yeast bacteria are put to work in such a medium as eggs, rich in nitrogen and poor in sugar, the yeast lives on the nitrogenous materials and produces salts of ammonia. These salts cause the death of the yeast bacteria, again by auto-intoxication.

After these facts had been demonstrated, Metchnikoff asked himself:

"If the lower plants (ferments and bacteria) die as the result of poisons produced by their own activity under certain conditions, do not the higher plants, such as the geranium, and higher animals, such as man, also produce poisons which are fatal to them?"

Our answer is: The animal that lives on normal food has the power within itself to control during its normal span of life the development and disposition of the waste products, or end-products, or poison products, which would sicken it or kill it if not controlled. When the conditions under which the animal lives are made abnormal, its powers of self-protection are correspondingly impaired; it loses its capacity to neutralize the destroying end-products of its own activity; it sickens or dies of auto-intoxication like the geranium.

One who lives on meat has to neutralize the waste products found in the flesh of the animal at the hour of its slaughter, in addition to neutralizing the waste products continually generating in his own body, thereby imposing upon his organs of elimination a double task while sustaining them with imperfect food.

When a tomato rots the process of decomposition by which it rots produces an end-product. When an egg rots it produces an end-product. These end-products are fatal to life. Any drug that permits us to make use of them, enables us not only to introduce the drug into the food of man but also to introduce bacterial poisons into that food. Anything that interferes with the activity of good bacteria or that enables bad bacteria to overdevelop in the body of an animal cannot have a good effect upon that animal.

We believe we have clearly shown that it is dangerous to denature or exhaust our food products by removing from them a vast number of vitalizing and controlling substances.

What scientist will say that nature's supply of mineral salts performs no function in preventing auto-intoxication by the poisonous end-products of life's processes? What scientist will say we do well when we tamper with our wheat and rice and barley and corn?

We believe we have shown that it is not only risky business but bad business to introduce into our foods other substances the conduct of which we can not explain to jury or judge.

Jury or judge can consider the figures tabulated at the beginning of these considerations.

Human intelligence can draw its own conclusions.

Shall we continue to gratify our eyes with unnatural color demands? Shall we continue to titillate our palates with artificial food creations and food refinement or—shall we continue to bury our children?

CHAPTER XVIII.

LABELS.

The menace of the food adulterators against the health of the nation will not end as long as money is to be made out of cheap adulterations or as long as people do not read and heed the fine print on food labels.

Why should honest food require a statement in small type printed along the border of its label where it is not likely to be noticed?

Foods that have been trifled with and shipped out of one state into another are obliged under the law to be labelled. But they are marked with inconspicuous phrases that have no meaning for the average consumer. These phrases are:

"A compound."
"Contains aluminum sulphate."
"Contains alum."
"Contains sulphur dioxide."
"Contains benzoate of sode."
"Contains SO²."
"Artificially flavored."
"Artificially colored."
"Contains sulphate of copper."
Etc., etc.

In Pennsylvania it is not legal to sell mushrooms bleached with sulphurous acid, and in North Carolina, Pennsylvania and Texas it is not legal to sell peas colored with sulphate of copper.

In all the other states of the union these foods and the hundred other foods containing chemical elements are served every day without argument or objection in the restaurants, hotels, boarding houses and homes of the people.

The packing case in which they are shipped from the manufacturer to the hotel keeper is plainly marked according to the law, but the individual dish served to the guest of the hotel shows no label.

The law makes you buy an individual drinking cup for a penny if you drink in the department stores or railway trains, but permits you to drink in the cafes, saloons and theatres from the glass that touches all lips, clean or foul.

We might take things into our own hands and insist when we go into the restaurant or hotel upon seeing the labels that were on the cans and bottles and cartons in which the foodstuffs were transported. If we made such a clamor we would be conspicuous, of course, but if we all did it, no one of us would be more conspicuous than the other. Thus by our own action we could discourage this debased food industry.

We have grasped an idea of the marvelously complex character of the organism we call the human body and we want to know henceforth what we are putting into that body.

Of what use is it for the law to require the candy manufacturer to inform the candy dealer that the penny candies sold to the children of the streets contain coal-tar dyes or artificial flavors made from oenanthic ether, valerianate ether, butyric ether, benzoic ether, acetic ether, formic ether, aldehydes, esters and chloroform? We do not know that the individual penny's worth taken from the legally labeled box contains these things.

The baker buys a tub of "process butter" made from reworked rancid butter and the tub is marked "renovated." He buys a tub of "compound" and it is so labeled He buys "chocolate color" for his icings which contains no chocolate. He buys "whip-it-up" for his egg effects and "egg color" for his cakes, and alum for his doughnuts and baking powder. He buys ethereal mixtures for his fruit flavors and a "synthetic compound" for his vanilla extract.

He buys preserved "fillers" for his pies and cakes.

He buys stiffening agents and substitutes for paraffin that will hold his ice cream firm for forty minutes in a temperature of eighty-five degrees.

All these things are properly labeled when they reach the baker. But layer cakes, his fancy cakes, his ice creams and his sweet-meats are not labeled. The little girls who make their purchases, and the mothers of these little girls have no means of knowing the ingredients of the things they buy and not knowing they do not suspect.

To what extent will egg color, whip-it-up, chocolate color, binding and stiffening agents, coal-tar dyes, ethereal flavors, fillers, facings, glazes, shellac, lacquer, compounds, bleaching solutions, liquid smoke, preservatives, etc., etc., nourish a nerve, build a bone, make a muscle or contribute to the life-sustaining power of the blood? These things are used by the bakers extensively and legally.

Wiley for years tried to have such abuses corrected but the "label interests" have successfully opposed the idea that we need better label laws.

The soda fountain serves synthetic fruit flavors, preservatives, artificial colors, stimulants and heart depressors, caffeine and acetanilid. They are all labeled on the original bottle, but the child that stands at the marble counter has no knowledge of the facts, although the proprietor of the soda fountain buys his materials from the manufacturer properly labeled.

If the label will tell us what we want to know let us cultivate a habit of looking at the label.

Let us find out why it is not politically necessary to change it.

Politics, like the signatures of chemists, cannot change those mortality records at Washington and in the background of our agitation for simple, honest, decent label laws, rise the spirits of a million little children gone from our homes.

CHAPTER XIX.

THE "POISON SQUAD."

"Poison Squads" are organized at regular intervals and healthy young men submit themselves to a diet of adulterated food in the interests of science.

After a period of five or six weeks the usual results are announced, frequently to the effect that the members of the squad "suffered no noticeable inconvenience and experienced no injury."

This report then appears in thousands of newspapers and quiets the public mind, disarms anxiety and suspicion. Sometimes it causes the cautious housewife to forget the necessity of watchfulness in selecting her kitchen supplies.

These "poison squads" never fight it out to the finish. The brave youths who are fed with doses of benzoate, borax, copper sulphate, sulphur dioxide, aluminum sulphate and the legal coal-tar dyes never take all of these delectable substances at any one time nor in any one test.

The "squad" is always confined to one drug, not tasting any other drug during its scientific experiment. Then before there is time for the subtle, slow-moving, insidious chemical to affect serious harm, the squad is disbanded and the food adulterator has been given "proof" that the cry against preservatives, food chemicals and mineral dyes is a bugaboo.

Now all the people in the world are not healthy young men, and all of them do not stop eating at the end of a test lasting five or six weeks. Some of them

are babies, some are school children, some are
nursing mothers, some are about to become mothers
and some have reached the age when natural vigor
is no longer sufficiently active to resist even temporary abuse.

In fact, we have organized "poison squads"
among little children and we do not disband those
squads until the children die.

Every time the law makes the use of a food
drug legal or every time it winks at an abuse that
denatures a food, it makes a permanent "poison
squad" of the whole country, not for a few experimental weeks, but for the life time of the individual.
All the little children of the country, whether their
parents realize it or not, are now in that "poison
squad." When the food-drugger puts his dose into
his product and sends it forth, he does not know
into whose hands it will fall nor the physical condition of the individual who will receive his medicated
wares.

We have already turned the whole country into
a test-tube with respect to the drugs we have noticed
here and though it is not realized it is none the less
an abomination. You are now in the national poison
squad. Little Helen and her 200,000 companions
have been graduated.

Concerning the national "poison squad" this
much is certain. Murders are being committed
through ignorance and selfishness in supplying unfit
food for the human family.

As life was given for some good purpose life's
efficiency should not be lessened by those who exploit the needs of life, particularly the natural foodstuffs upon which life depends.

Of the 250 infants that die before they are one
year old out of every thousand born, and of the

countless score of adults that die before their time, many lives could be saved if the food manufacturer could be made to realize the responsibility he takes upon himself when he assumes that it is his right to feed the nation with no other object before him than the profit to himself. All murders are not picturesque. The slow-moving, subtle, insidious, undermining of the health of man, woman or child is murder.

Individuals have no right to debase food products, the natural result of which is to bring about degeneration, ill health, and perhaps death, to those who depend upon impoverished foods.

Self-slaughter is given the widest possible publicity. The subtle slaughtering of the race is given no publicity, but is passed by without notice, because the nation neither knows the facts nor realizes their results.

To hide the truth by refusing it publicity is to be guilty of whatever murder is involved in robbing the people's foodstuffs of the elements necessary to sustain life.

If life is sacred everything upon which life depends is sacred and the juggling, refining or denaturing of man's food supply is sacrilege.

We are asking that the schools and colleges should teach the relative viciousness and baseness of crime so that public opinion may proclaim that mob murders and self-murders are the most cowardly and least defensible of all offenses. Let us also demand that they teach with their anatomy and hygiene the meaning of the presence of proteins, carbohydrates, fats and minerals in the diet, so that any commercial effort to interfere with these elements for the sake of profit may be resented as a crime against the sacredness of life.

That the destroyers of their own lives are denied church burial by three great branches of the Christion religion indicates that the idea of the sacredness of human life is universal. It adds one more indictment against public apathy and private greed where foodstuffs are concerned.

If the average man, though a stranger, will afford succor to his fellow to prevent a death by violence, would he not endeavor to prevent our modern food crimes if he realized even remotely the enormity of those crimes, as shown in their consequences?

If, at sea, men of wealth and power surrender their lives calmly and heroically, while their maid servants and the women of the steerage are given place in the lifeboats can we on shore not understand the duty of the living?

Why should we respond with reverence and tears to the acts of brave souls when they serenely yield their lives for the public good, and then refuse to pick up our own little fragment of public duty lying at our feet, because we do not find it gleaming with the gold of romance?

If we honor thousands of noble men and women who spend their lives at the hospital bedside to bring the sick back again to health, is it not nobler still to fight beforehand against preventable disease?

Are we not all active and responsible agents in the great national department of health?

Who can deny that the hour has come when we must, positively and actively, demand honest food?

CHAPTER XX.

"KEEPING" FOODS.

But you say, if we talk to the cereal dealer or the miller about natural breakfast foods and natural whole wheat meal and natural corn, etc., he tells us that it is impossible to successfully market breakfast food or whole wheat meal or any of the other grains in their natural state, because they become stale and spoil, or, as in the case of natural brown rice during the hot germinating months, they are subject to weevil infestation.

The dealer states that when the housekeeper buys a stale package or a package containing weevils, she forthwith condemns the product as a class, and will have nothing more to do with it, henceforth forever.

But the attitude of the cracker baker, the coffee roaster, the egg dealer, the milk man and the bread baker, is different toward his equally perishable product. These become stale with age, but the dealer does not refuse to put them on the market. The coffee man sees to it that his roasted coffee reaches the housekeeper fresh and fragrant; the cracker baker sees that his crackers reach the housekeeper fresh and crisp, and the bread man makes arrangements to have his bread reach the housekeeper while it is fresh

Coffee, bread, eggs and milk are perishable products and in consequence, they are prepared as needed.

Wheat will keep for years, so will barley and corn and oats. Rice with a little care will keep in the same way. The grains do not spoil until they are ground and then they spoil in the hot, germinating months only.

The Bureau of Etomology, United States Department of Agriculture, has gone to some trouble to discover the processes, whereby natural brown rice might be kept free from weevil infestation. It's the old story. Man, in his attempt to improve on the wise provisions of mother nature, usually meets with failure.

The scientist is puzzled indeed, when he is obliged to begin in the middle, and work both ways at once. Science will probably find no means of preventing the weevil from attacking natural brown rice. Nature has provided the means, and science, up to this writing, spurns nature's device.

In order to protect the rice for us, until we require it for our food, nature covers it with a hard shell, in which the rice keeps indefinitely.

Thousands of years ago, Pharaoh took notice of this fact, and for the benefit of his people, he stored rice in the granaries of Egypt, permitting the grain to remain in the shell in which nature had placed it.

Thus the grains were held unwinnowed for years, to provide against periods of famine. Weevils did not worry the Egyptians, and scientists were not required to devise chemical methods of protecting the grain, because man instead of defying nature, co-operated with her laws.

Nowadays we winnow the rice in a heap, thereby exposing it to the attacks of insects, against which nature had protected it with that shell.

Man builds a shell in the form of a glass bottle, or jar, or a tin can, around any animal or vegetable product which he wishes to preserve against the attack of living organisms. He knows that if he takes the shell off his product, by removing it from the bottle, jar or can, the laws of nature will operate, and destroy his product.

If we wish uncontaminated oat meal, corn meal, wheat meal, barley or rice, we must not prepare a year's supply in advance. We must prepare it at reasonable intervals, and in harmony with nature's laws.

By grinding more frequently in smaller quantities, we may bring them to the people as nature intended them to be used.

The mere fact that somebody has invested money in a business for profit does not impose upon the world an obligation to eat denatured breakfast foods and lifeless bread in order that some breakfast food concern or miller or baker may declare a larger dividend.

The world wants more energy and ingenuity applied to the problem of its needs. It wants that problem solved as the coffee man, the cracker man, the bread man, the egg man and the milk man have solved it.

If more coffee mills were put to the work of grinding wheat and corn and barley and oats at home, it would soon become unnecessary to hunt for arguments to induce the miller and the baker to change his present methods!

With a coffee mill at home and a bag of wheat or a bag of oats or a bag of corn we could make our own honest meal; and when we begin to do that

simple thing, the great American breaa eater, the
child of the poor, will have sturdier limbs, rosier
cheeks, brighter eyes and a happier heart.

CHAPTER XXI.

THE PROCESSION OF LITTLE WHITE CASKETS.

More than one hundred and fifty-four thousand little white caskets going out of the homes of this nation in one year! How might many of those deaths have been prevented?

From the day of birth, and prior to the day of birth, children's diseases are brought about—with the exception of specific blood poison and the diseases that follow in the trail of parental vice—by errors in feeding.

If the child is started right, and this means beginning before birth, it will possess the vitality necessary to resist disease as well as the power within itself of appropriating normal food for the requirements of its developing body.

The mother's milk is the ideal food for the child. Every mother should make heroic efforts to nurse her baby. Many mothers who are normally fit, fail to discharge this tremendous obligation to the child because they are ignorant of the fact that upon it depends largely the child's future.

Euchres, teas, theatres, club life cannot compensate for the loss caused by compelling the child to depend on artificial sources for its food.

Infants nursed by healthy mothers are stronger than infants nursed on the bottle. Bottle-fed babies often look well and normal when compared with breast-fed babies, but the future discloses the difference. Because a child grows fat on an artificial

diet does not mean that that diet is giving it resistance to rickets, swollen glands, predisposition to
disease, etc.

Cow's milk is not the same as mother's milk.

Certified cow's milk can be modified to resemble
physiologically mother's milk but the difference
is still a menace to the health of the infant.

If there is doubt about the cleanliness of the
milk, doubt about its freedom from pathogenic bacteria, it might be pasteurized, but pasteurized milk
is justifiable for one reason only and that reason
a doubtful one. It is better, perhaps, to give the
child tubercle bacilli or other disease-breeding organisms after they have been destroyed by pasteurization than to give them these living organisms in
raw milk.

Certified milk costs five cents per quart more
than the average raw milk. That investment of
five cents imposes no real hardship on the poorest
father or mother. In New York City the most
wretched and underpaid laborer finds his ten cents
for whiskey. If he is a father let him rather put
that money into milk protection for his child.

Raw cow's milk from healthy animals properly
certified and fed to the infant at blood heat is essential to the well being of the child that knows no in-
timacy with its mother's breast.

When milk is pasteurized or subjected to a temperature above 98⅔ degrees it undergoes a chemical
change. Its albuminoids and mineral constituents so
necessary to the construction of the child's bone,
tissue and blood become partially disorganized and
the casseine is toughened.

Human caseine acted upon by the gastric juice
of the infant's stomach is reduced to tender flecks
which readily submit to digestive action. Cow's

milk, even when raw, forms large curds. When pasteurized, the curds offer still greater resistance to the feeble digestion of the baby. Still, perhaps it is better to feed the child pasteurized milk than to feed it unclean milk. Pasteurization does not work miracles in dirty milk for the reason that neither pasteurization nor boiling can kill the decomposition products or poisonous end-products of the bacteria, although the bacteria that produce these poisons are themselve destroyed.

On artificial diets, including condensed milk, containing cane sugar the infant cannot escape constipation. For this reason fruit juice should be given to the baby three or four times a day. The freshly pressed, carefully strained juice of oranges is the ideal fruit juice for the infant. A teaspoonful of such orange juice three times a day is the most important addition to the artificially fed baby's diet. Never give fruit juice immediately after or immediately before feeding. Never use juice from fruit containing bruises or green fruit or over-ripe fruit. See to it that it is scrupulously strained so that none of the fruit pulp is swallowed by the infant. Even the child fed from its mother's breast is benefited by the fruit juice addition to its food. The acid of the fruit almost instantly decomposes in the child's stomach and is converted into alkaline salts of potassium and calcium. Do not fear such "acid" for the child.

The healthy mother who has not sufficient milk for her baby, provided the milk she has be of good quality, is not justified in refusing the child what little she has. Such human milk is important and when supplemented by properly modified cow's milk, the infant so fed will enjoy advantages over the infant fed entirely on the bottle. If one had a half

loaf of good bread in the bread box would she throw
that half loaf away because it was not a whole loaf,
and substitute in its stead a whole loaf of poor
bread? The doctor's advice is the advice to follow
because the responsibility is the doctor's responsibility. He will usually agree with the well-dis-
posed mother that it is better for her to nurse her
baby with the milk she has and to make up the
deficiency artificially than not to nurse her baby at
all. On a diet of debased food nature will shut off
the mother's milk supply. The mother who would
nurse her precious babe must eat food acceptable to
nature.

When the child cries he often wants a teaspoonful
of water. He never needs distilled water. Beware
of distilled water, not only for the child, but for
the adult. It is mineral-free and mineral-hungry.
We must not let it feed upon the child.

Neither infants nor children should have cane
sugar in their diet, as it is now made, although honest, old-fashioned cane sugar was a natural and a
nutritious food. The sugar-bowl on the table
of the twentieth century home is one of the most
deadly curses laid by ignorance upon child-life. The
child's stomach makes its own sugar. Every ounce
of starch he consumes must be converted into sugar
before digestion. Mothers of children must be made
to realize that artificial sweets sap the child's body
of its most indispensable substances and bring about
disorder of the bones and teeth. The child's love
for sweets is to be satisfied with the sweets organized
for him by all-generous nature plus human intelligence. He gets these sweets not only in a harmless,
but in a beneficial form, in the fruits of the earth and
at two and a half years of age there is not one ripe
fruit which the child cannot digest and assimilate in

moderate quantities. Even the date will impose no tax upon the digestion after the third year unless he over-eats. Honey, sap maple syrup and old-fashioned molasses, with unrefined cane sugar, contain the tissue salts of the cane, tree and flower, the iron and calcium, that nature put there. Such forms of sweets are natural and good. Candy prepared from them is good candy for the child. Yes, this advocates the use of "impure" sugar for there is no such thing as pure sugar in nature. The sugar found in vegetables, fruits, reeds, trees, etc., is unrefined, just as the starch in these things is unrefined. This is as it should be, and we should not allow any industry, however powerful or privileged, to take anything out of our food which nature intended to be there. Chemically pure sugar, $C_{12} H_{22} O_{11}$, is not found in nature. It is the product of the laboratory, not of God.

The writer's children eat no artificial sweets. They are happy, very, very happy. There is touching pathos in their childish efforts to dissuade their little companions not to eat the evil or worthless things that are everywhere offered them in mistaken kindness, or in exchange for their pennies. They call the date, apple, orange, berry, banana, fig, prune, plum and peach, "God's candy." They see that nobody gives "doggie or kitty or bird or horse or chicks" cane sugar. They understand. Their lives are not empty. From the very beginning they grasp the necessity of drawing a line between good and evil, between the essential and the non-essential, between the moment's pleasure and its consequence.

CHAPTER XXII.

WHAT TO FEED THE CHILD.

What should our children eat, if we do as well by them as the farmer does by his prize poultry and cattle?

The following suggestions are the result of intimate study of child life covering a period of many years.

Some persons believe that the child must have the mumps, measles, croup, etc., and actually go so far as to expose children to such diseases under the mistaken idea that as the child has to get sick in such fashion anyhow, it is better to have it done with and over as soon as possible. Children properly fed need not get sick. They will resist the so-called children's diseases, just as the horse resists tuberculosis.

The diet that follows presents the fortification that has withstood for more than six years all the assaults of infant ills in the writer's own family.

FOR CHILDREN THREE YEARS AND OVER.

BREAKFAST MONDAY.

One-half small grape fruit or one-quarter large grape fruit, or sliced ripe peaches, ripe raspberries, blackberries, strawberries or ripe cantaloupe.

Natural brown rice and certified milk.

Whole wheat bread and butter.

BREAKFAST TUESDAY.

Scraped raw apple, baked apple or whole raw

apple, skin and all, when the child can be trusted
to use its teeth properly.

Whole wheat meal porridge and certified milk.

Whole wheat bread, sweet butter and honey.

BREAKFAST WEDNESDAY.

Juice of whole orange.

Old-fashioned, unsteamed, unscoured oat meal
with certified milk.

Whole wheat bread and butter.

BREAKFAST THURSDAY.

Stewed dates.

Poached egg on whole wheat toast.

Certified milk.

Whole wheat bread and pure maple syrup.

BREAKFAST FRIDAY.

Stewed prunes.

Unpearled barley with certified milk.

Whole wheat bread.

BREAKFAST SATURDAY.

Grape fruit, orange juice, apple or any other
fruit.

Old-fashioned, undegerminated corn meal and
certified milk.

Whole wheat bread.

BREAKFAST SUNDAY.

Stewed figs or apple sauce.

Natural wheat food or breakfast food made of
undebased, unimpoverished, unscoured, unpolished,
unsoaked, unbleached barley, oats or wheat with
certified milk and a sprinkle of old-fashioned, unsul-
phured brown sugar if it can be found.

Whole wheat muffins made with raisins, currants
or dates.

OBSERVATIONS:

These breakfast combinations are not arbitrary. They are intended as suggestions based on a knowledge of the meaning of proteins, carbohydrates, fats and mineral salts. With these combinations, the child will not be tempted to over-eat. The appetite will not be abnormal. To-day he may not eat bread in addition to his cereals. To-morrow he may not · be content with less than one slice of bread; or he may want two. His needs will guide him. Any variations that normal taste demands, or that will relieve monotony, or any breakfast food made from the honest raw grain, containing all of the grain, can be substituted as desired. The fruit may consist solely of apples with splendid results.

The necessary potassium and calcium salts are found in the fruit suggested. Phosphorus, chlorine, iron, sodium, calcium, sulphur, silica, magnesium and manganese are found in the natural grains, milk and bread suggested.

If the butter is not fresh, the child is better off without it. The less butter he eats the better.

DINNER MONDAY.

Soups made of a combination of four or five fresh vegetables and greens, such as onions, parsley, carrots, spinach, parsnips, celery or celery tops.

Potato baked in its skin. When the skin is baked crisp the child can eat it with impunity. If soggy, it is better to let not only the skin but the potato alone.

Poached egg or an egg cooked in its shell for ten minutes in water at 160 degrees Fahrenheit.

Endives, lettuce, crisp celery or greens of any kind.

Three or four dates or one or two figs or three or four ripe olives or a bunch of grapes in season.

DINNER TUESDAY.

Thick lentil soup (not more than one-half cupful).

Stewed carrots served in the water in which they are cooked, thickened with whole wheat meal.

Greens.

Whole wheat bread.

Stewed fresh rhubarb or apple sauce, or any ripe fruit.

DINNER WEDNESDAY.

Stewed onion juice with the onions.

Poached egg or egg cooked ten minutes at 160 degrees.

Stewed parsnips served in own sauce.

Creamed fresh peas or tender corn on cob.

Fruit or ripe olives.

A slice of whole wheat bread and honey.

DINNER THURSDAY.

Thick bean soup.

Stewed fresh spinach served in own sauce.

Any vegetable combination such as turnips, fresh beets, parsnips or potatoes.

Barley cakes or oat cakes.

Apples, apple pudding or apple sauce.

DINNER FRIDAY.

Soup made of greens with barley or rice or both.

Dried peas, dried beans or dried lentils soaked ten hours and cooked ten hours.

Old-fashioned sun-dried apples or sun-dried apricots if the fresh variety is not in season.

Whole wheat bread.

DINNER SATURDAY.

Vegetable soup.

Natural brown rice with custard sauce.

Greens.

Sliced fresh pineapple, sliced fresh peaches, berries or cantaloupe.

Whole wheat bread and three or four ripe olives.

DINNER SUNDAY.

Chicken soup with boiled or roast chicken.

Creamed onions, cauliflower or Brussels sprouts.

Greens.

Baked banana with light cake containing eggs.

Grape juice.

Whole wheat bread and maple syrup.

A thin film of fresh peanut butter on such days as eggs are not served is a good addition to bread. The peanut butter must be fresh. When stale, the fatty acids of which it is composed split up and produce an irritant substance called acrolein, which is a solvent of flesh dangerous to child or adult life. Nuts may be served only when ground or when the child has been taught to thoroughly masticate them. A little grated Parmesan, Roman or whole milk cheese can be sprinkled over potatoes, turnips, carrots or bread as an occasional addition to this diet. It must be remembered that cheese, like eggs, beans, peas, lentils and milk, is nitrogen (meat). Nitrogen is indispensable though too much is bad.

The child may be allowed occasionally fresh fruit jelly or fresh fruit jam, both of which are semi-natural sweets. The living ferments necessary to perfect digestion are provided through the medium of the raw greens and raw fruits as suggested.

EVENING LUNCH UP TO SIX YEARS.

MONDAY.

Certified milk and whole wheat bread or oaten crackers.

TUESDAY.

Certified milk and whole bread or undegerminated corn porridge.

WEDNESDAY.

Certified milk and whole wheat bread.

This simple combination should be repeated or intelligently varied at the other evening meals, which should be the lightest of the day.

OBSERVATION:

Between six and ten eggs per week depending on the vigor of the child should be consumed between its third and ninth year. At five years six eggs constitute the outside limit. Fresh olive oil can be used in moderate quantities, a teaspoonful, for instance, with greens or salads.

The things which the child should not eat are: artificial sweets (robbed of the cane salts, explained later) artificially colored and artificially flavored; grease gravy, fried foods of any kind; sulphur-bleached apricots, apples, peaches, pears, raisins or prunes; chili sauce, catsup, pickles, condiments or any other food containing vinegar; vegetables that have lost their soluble salts by boiling or stewing in water subsequently poured down the waste-pipe; boiled meats; fried meats, liver, kidney, hard boiled eggs unless the latter are pulverized; molasses or other forms of sugar bleached with sulphurous acid, cookies, ginger bread and taffy made from such molasses; all food artificially colored with any of the coal-tar dyes, all canned foods unless the cans are lacquered, all bake shop or drug store ice cream made from "loose milk," gelatine, ethereal flavors and artificial colors; all factory or fancy cakes contaminated with aluminum sulphate, fillers, ethereal flavors, stearine, artificial jellies, coal-tar colors, etc.

Ice cream made at home from certified milk or a mixture of certified milk and wholesome cream is permitted in small quantities but it should be eaten slowly and not on top of a full meal. Coffee and tea are not permissable.

Dr. C. K. Taylor, studying the effect of coffee drinking on 464 school children, found that about 29 per cent of those children drank no coffee, while 71 per cent drank from one to two or more cups a day. Dr. Taylor found that as regards physical measurements, the children who drank coffee averaged from one and one-half to more than four pounds less in weight, and from one-half inch to more than one inch less in height, than the children who abstained from coffee. They were also found to have an average of three pounds less in hand strength, than the children who never drank coffee.

Dr. Taylor concludes that it seems likely that the regular drinking of coffee by children, has an effect which seems to make the child less "fit" physically as well as mentally, than those who do not use coffee.

Under the above diet, constipation and other bowel and stomach disorders are impossible unless the child is permitted to stuff. If left to his own inclinations with such food he will manifest no tendency to stuff. His perfectly nourished body asserts no unnatural craving and as a result he will not gorge himself. It is absurd to assume that with such a bill of fare the child is being deprived of the hundred and one "innocent and delightful tidbits" which have been inherited from hundreds of years of grandmotherdom.

When it can be shown that nourished upon such food the child is perfectly happy and that defective vision, defective teeth, lusterless eyes, pinched cheeks, underdeveloped limbs, low resistance to diseases are all avoided, and sturdy, sparkling, buoyant, energetic childhood is produced, intelligent mother-love can have no patience with those who assert that the child should have his share of the world's artificial and ridiculous luxuries.

Perhaps the most remarkable phenomenon to be observed under such a diet, is the utter unwillingness of the child to eat between meals. He makes no clamor for food of any kind before dinner or in the afternoon.

Prior to the age of six the child should go to bed at six o'clock and should sleep in all kinds of weather in a cold room with the windows wide open. The best food in the world will accomplish little if the child is obliged to breathe the same air twice.

After the sixth year the child may have his evening meal with father and mother, continuing to observe the rules of simplicity regardless of the manner in which the table is set or the character of foods upon it.

If the one condition under which little Helen's father and mother could have their darling restored to their arms consisted in a promise to feed her properly, could they meet that condition?

This book is written for those who would answer, yes!

If the Sunday School picnic or the birthday party or the circus excursion includes factory ice cream made of "loose milk," bacteria-infected gelatine, with coal-tar dye and ethereal flavors the child should not go.

This book demands revolution. If its demands be not heeded, the alternative is that we can continue to murder our children. We can continue to bury those who die before their time. Let us demand imperatively that our representatives and our legislators prove that they know the truths written here before they swear fidelity to their trust as servants of the people.

We must have a legally standardized loaf of whole wheat bread made of certified whole wheat meal. Otherwise, the adulterator will use the creamy color of the honest loaf as a mask to conceal inferiority and dirt. The white bread maker will then point to his immaculate loaf free from the faintest speck of color and triumphantly contrast its "chastity" with the possibility of dirt and defilement in the darker loaf. The people will look with suspicion upon the creamy product, develop anxiety over it, lose faith in it and again abandon it in favor of the "clean" white loaf. We have certified milk, certified drugs, certified checks with which to pay for them. The certified loaf or the home-made loaf with love kneaded into its heart will be the standard bread of America when you so resolve.

There would be no reason for condemning fruits or vegetables in tin cans if the canners would devise some means of preventing erosion in the tins by the action of enzymes or the action of the fruit and vegetable acids. Tin is not one of the benevolent minerals. Neither is lead. These are not found in the human body except as we introduce them into our stomachs with canned food in the shape of salts of tin and lead. Arsenic in cheap tin plate readily passes over into solution with the contents of the can. It is the duty of the canner to safe-guard his canned products from these poisons.

The canner is now seriously aroused, over this question. His chemists are striving to find a way to prevent the formation of tin salts in vegetables

and fruits. Until he can guarantee his product free
from tin in solution no child should be permitted
to eat any food that has been packed in tin.

CHAPTER XXIII.

INCREASING DEATH RATE.

Great have been the changes of the past few years.

People are thinking in terms of the telegraph, the telephone, the "wireless," the aeroplane, the submarine. Men have invented new machines and the new machines have turned upon them and have created new men. Men now live in wider distances and think in larger circles.

But we have not only the telescope but the microscope. Life has not only become more extensive, but more intensive. We see the power of the little things, the hidden forces of life.

The poisonous phosphorus match that destroyed by necrosis the bones of the men and women who made it; that, thoughtlessly put into the mouth of a child, mysteriously occasioned its sickness or death, yes, even the phosphorus match has been swept out of the land or, is to be!

It was common, insignificant, yet it dealt death subtly and slowly. Other commonplace dangers of the kitchen are no longer regarded as trifles, but are now being investigated and catalogued for just what they are.

A great life assurance society has established a Department of Conservation through which to teach men, women and children the simple fundamentals of life.

This is indeed an age of high pressure and of rapid living. Thomas A. Edison has declared that he has already lived 110 years because for thirty or forty years he has been able to work from fifteen to eighteen hours a day. Here and there a human machine can stand the rack and wear of such a heavy strain, but as the Equitable Life Assurance Society tells us, it is useless for a man who is equipped to carry a hundred pounds of steam with safety to try to carry two hundred pounds. This is why so many men from forty to fifty are dying of kidney, heart or arterial troubles.

Within one week the New York newspapers in the year 1912 reported the unexpected deaths of three prominent men who were living this intense business life in addition to the strain of their social duties. The world calls these tragedies "sudden" deaths. They were not sudden deaths.

A few years ago a crowded express train broke through a bridge and destroyed a hundred lives. An investigation showed that the strands in the great cable of the bridge had been giving away one by one until the final strain.

Few deaths are sudden. The daily routine of life, the habits of mind, of work, of worry, of recreation, are the daily jar and strain of the strands in the great cables of the human bridge, which are thus slowly broken until some day under a heavier strain than usual the structure falls. It was not a sudden accident; it was the inevitable end. Physical bankruptcy is quite similar to financial bankruptcy. As long as the daily and yearly expenditure of strength and vitality exceeds ever so little the income of repair and recuperation, just so long will there be certainty that the "run" on the Bank of Health will finally close its doors.

A man is as old as his arteries. The man of
forty, fifty or even sixty years of age should not
have arteries lacking in elasticity. When the young
man has the arteries of the old man, it is because his
habits of eating and working, thinking and drinking
have crowded too many years into his short span of
existence, giving him the arteries of the aged.

Nothing will so soon produce hardening of the
arteries as impure food. As the arteries harden,
a little extra pressure produces a break like the
snapping of a strand in the cable.

This condition can be prevented by supplying the
heart and its electric batteries, or nerve cells, with
proper material to repair the waste and continual
drain upon them.

The blood obtains its nourishment from the
stomach, and its oxygen from the lungs. It relieves
itself of waste products by means of the kidneys and
spleen. Steady, rhythmical heart-beats are brought
about by pure food in right quantities.

Right thinking, moderation in eating and drinking, regular daily exercise in the open air and proper
bathing, with food of a proper kind will long with-
stand the attacks of disease and death.

The Equitable Life Assurance gives us a number
of highly significant facts to consider.

DEATH RATE.

	1909	1910
Richmond	20.7	22.6
Portland, Ore.	9.8	11.0
Memphis	20.1	21.4
Washington	19.0	19.6
Minnesota	10.7	12.3
Albany	17.6	19.4
New York	16.0	16.0

New Orleans 20.2   21.3
Chicago 14.6   15.1
Denver 17.0   16.4
Los Angeles 13.7   14.0
Birmingham 18.2   19.5

The difference in these death rates was due, according to the Equitable Life Assurance Society's comment to difference in age distribution, local conditions and VARYING VALUE OF PUBLIC HEALTH SERVICE. The average death rate for the year 1910 in the cities mentioned was 16.8.

If we should teach these thirteen cities the meaning of food, how to feed their children, how to feed their adults; if we should teach them the worthlessness of impoverished and denatured food, if we should point out to them a short cut back to nature, the death rate of 16.8 in one generation would be reduced to less than 6.8.

Thoughtless people sometimes say to the writer in his public addresses: "Well, if our food is so imperfect, why do people live longer than they did in years gone by?" There is only one answer to that question: We banished yellow fever and other filth diseases by cleaning house. We no longer drink sewage on a large scale. Federal and state laws are invoked continually to protect us from this evil. Our Health Departments do not permit us to pile the city streets with decaying refuse. If with our advance in sanitation we had given the same attention to our food supply we would have an inspiring story to tell.

In the meantime we do not know that people live longer now-a-days (the average length of life is 44 years) for there are no statistics with which to make comparison and the Equitable figures, just quoted, show an increase in deaths, not a decrease.

CHAPTER XXIV.

A man might be compared to a steam boiler constructed of many plates of various metals, differing in strength and thickness. Under low pressure such a boiler might endure for a long time. Inside the boiler some of the plates are slowly attracting deposits. The aluminum plate resists the action of acids, copper plate resists rust, but the iron plate is corroding and becoming thinner. Finally the pressure in the boiler is raised a little and the boiler gives way—at its weakest spot.

Man is a victim of diseases known by many different names according to the position and character of the weakest spot.

All disease springs from pollution or impoverishment of the blood stream, and manifests itself in the weak spot of the individual.

In one case we may have locomotor ataxia, in another a sore eye; in one case Bright's disease, in another rheumatism, and so on through thousands of disorders.

The man who raises pigeons insists on whole red wheat and whole corn for their food to prevent diseases of any kind. His object is to protect the weak spot.

All the while fixed laws are at work in the human body. Whatever we put into the body will produce results according to the quality and quantity of the elements ingested. Hydrocyanic acid administered to a Monogolian in China and hydrocyanic acid administered to a New Yorker in the Rockefeller Institute, 10,000 miles distant, will produce similar results. Morphine, digitalis, cocoaine act in Austria just as they act in Brazil. The proper quantity of certain mineral elements taken in the form of foods organized by nature will produce the same results in Bombay as in London.

The school girls of to-day are destined to be the mothers of the race ten or twenty years hence. The study of foods and their relationship to health belongs to the school room.

The Department of Domestic Economy in all schools could take up this question under three heads —honest food, denatured food, adulterated food.

Professor Lewis B. Allyn of the Department of Chemistry, Massachusetts State Normal School, Westfield, Massachusetts, has shown what wonderful benefits the town of Westfield has derived from the study which the school children of that town have given to the subject of adulterated food.

Food should be studied with regard to the value of the food elements which man removes by his so-called processes of refinement.

Such lessons taught in all the schools of America would give this great land in one generation a new race of men.

For a practical demonstration of these things let us put ten cages in the school-yard, or on the roof of the schoolhouse. Into each of five of these cages place four chickens, which the school children may themselves feed.

The chickens in cage No. 1 will be fed whole corn, whole oats, natural rice, whole wheat, un-pearled barley, grass or greens of any kind, and water. The children will note that on this diet the chickens in cage No. 1 will be proud and spirited. Their feathers will be brilliant, their flesh firm and their bodies well developed.

The same children will feed the chickens in cage No. 2 with equal mixtures of whole grains and denatured grains, the remainder of the diet being the same. They will note that at the end of a period of six months there will be marked superiority in appearance among the chickens in cage No. 1.

The same children will feed the chickens in cage No. 3 with pearled barley, polished rice, processed oats, degerminated corn meal and doughballs made of white flour and water with the same quantity of greens fed to chickens in cages No. 1 and No. 2. In a few months, the marked physical degeneracy of the health of these chickens will teach the children its own lesson.

The same children will feed chickens in cages No. 4 with meat pulp from which the mineral salts have been extracted by leaching in distilled water. In addition to this they shall be fed all the soda crackers, white biscuits, ginger bread, ginger snaps, fancy cakes, white bread and candy they can eat, plus water with the usual quantity of gravel and greens. Their condition in a few months will be eloquently suggestive to the children.

The same children will feed the chickens in cage No. 5 with white bread, white biscuits, white crackers and cakes, caramels, pickles, ethereal soda water and other fancy drinks, with gravel but without greens. As the feathers of these chickens begin to droop and the chickens begin to huddle in the corners of their cage seeking the darkness, miserable, thin and sick, the lesson of the relationship of food to animal life will be taught.

At this stage of the experiment the healthy chickens in cage No. 1 will be transferred to cage No. 6 and there they will be fed on the diet of cage No. 5 until they begin to show the same symptoms of dissolution and disease.

The chickens of cages No. 2, No. 3, No. 4, No. 5 will then be put in cages No. 7, No. 8, No. 9, No. 10 and will be fed on the natural, undebased, unimpoverished, undenatured diet of cage No. 1. The children will see the sick chickens recover rapidly and thoroughly, and they will go through life with a thoroughly learned lesson, and when they assume the responsibility of home life they will not abandon the laws of nature in the pursuit of some capricious food-ornament at the expense of the health, happiness and welfare of those dependent upon them.

CHAPTER XXV.

THE HUNGRY SOIL.

The Nile floods raised grain for the Egyptians in such abundance that the land of Egypt became the "granary of the nation." Along the valley of the Nile the staff of life sprang up out of the thin film of mineral silt and clay which the swollen river laid at the feet of the Egyptians. The Nile performed a function, the significance of which was not understood, but the results of which were remarkable. The Egyptian bread was made of sound, vigorous, undegerminated, undemineralized grain and the soundness of the grain passed into the bodies of the men who fed upon it.

When the Nile annually overflowed the land of Egypt, it did not bring with it unnatural chemical fertilizer or the putrefactions of manure. The Nile flood brought from the hills into the valleys tons of mineral rock in dust-like particles or held in solution by the waters, which replaced in the soil the vitalizing mineral elements which the vegetation of the preceding year had taken from it. With the unlocking of the flood gates of the Nile the bread problem of all ages should have been solved, and as if to emphasize the meaning of stone in the destiny of man, the Egyptians piled stone upon stone in pyramids that will not die.

The Sphinx is no longer silent. She tells the weaklings of the twentieth century that back there in the darkness of humanity's cradle lies the secret

that will make men free and strong and mighty—the
secret of stone. The certainty of honest bread and
plenty of it means more to the people who live on
the surface of this planet than poet or philosopher
has ever taught. Honest bread grown from lava
rock, means for the children of men, time, inclina-
tion and power through which to express the almost
infinite potentialities of the human family. Let us
visit our quarries of volcanic stone and our beds of
volcanic mud so that we may grasp the meaning they
have for the feeble nations of the earth.

In its precious freight of fertilizing rock the
Nile flood poured lavish treasures upon the people
of Egypt which might have taught humanity a lesson that would have prevented the bread famines
of Ireland, India, Russia and China. There can be
no funeral pyres by the roadside or on the outskirts
of the camp, the starved bodies of men will not be
burned to the god of ignorance, the vulture will no
longer hover over human carrion labeled "offered to
lifeless bread and too little of it," when the lesson
of the Nile is learned.

Somebody has said that in England two million
people are hungry all the time and that slowly but
surely the fibre of the nation is eaten into by a subtle and insidious starvation. Another has said that
England with her people struggling for bread cannot get sufficient young men for her armies physically able to stand the rigors of five years' service in
her tropical possessions.

The hunger of the soil for mineral rock was not
known in the valley of the Nile, and the pyramids
tell us that the hunger of men for honest bread free
from the pollutions of the stable will not be known
in the valley of twentieth century enlightenment.

It has been noted that in volcanic soil and on mountainous lands man harvests wonderful crops. Blindly turning his back upon these phenomena, he takes the by-products of the slaughter house and the dung of the pig pen in the form of ammonia and phosphate fertilizers, and with such so-called plant food, he rots and sours and pollutes the earth, inoculating the roots of his plants with the fountains of putrefaction. The vigorous plant for a while may resist disease just as the vigorous man for a while may resist typhoid, but soil overfed on decomposing nitrogenous compounds, uric acid, etc., and underfed on the mineral food which misguided superstition has falsely believed to be abundantly present in all earth, inevitably produces physiological discord in vegetable life. The ignorant farmer, hidebound by the traditions of his father and inspired by the desperate teachings of a misguided science, looks up into the diseased leaves instead of down at the starved roots, and believes that by spraying his feeble plants with germicides and fancy serums, he can kill blight and scale and fungi and cut worms and weevils and the other morbid growths and parasites which deprave and destroy the fruits of the earth.

Along the foothills of Maine and in all land contiguous to volcanic formation where the rains carry the digested or broken mineral stone to the soil, nature produces crops so lusty and vigorous that they resist plant-sickness and men fed on the unrefined or unjuggled crops of such soil resist body-sickness. Mineral rock of volcanic origin abounds all over the earth, rich in iron, calcium, magnesium, potassium, phosphorus, silica, manganese. The rock formations of Washington, Oregon, Colorado and Maine emphasize the secret of the Nile

Why is manure fertilizer impossible on an extended basis? For the reason that no farmer is able to grow enough forage on poor land to feed enough stock to make enough manure to make that poor land rich. Any farmer, who on any farm in the United States can produce enough feed and forage to feed enough live stock to produce enough manure to turn that farm from a non-productive state into a high state of cultivation, can raise the dead to life. One farmer may procure enough feed, cotton seed meal, bran and shorts from another farm to feed animals which will produce manure to promote in his particular farm a high state of fertility. What is taken from one farm may produce temporary results in another farm, but in the meantime where are the farms that thus squander their own manure going to get sufficient soil-food to keep their own soil from exhaustion? By the unnatural manure method of fertilizing, one farm may be maintained in a state of fertility at the expense of ten adjacent farms which are required to exhaust themselves in order to lend their strength to the invalid farm.

Dr. C. G. Hopkins says, "In nearly all sections of the country a farmer can be found here and there —sometimes one in ten, and sometimes only one in a hundred—who feeds all the crops that he raises and also all that he can buy at reasonably low prices from his neighbors, supplementing all this with purchased bran, shorts, oil meal, cotton seed meal, etc., and is thus able to produce sufficient manure to maintain or even to increase the fertility of his own farm at the expense of some other farm."

If keeping live stock with its continuous performance method of eating the fruits of the soil in order to produce manure for the soil, constituted a natural method of bringing up bad soil to good condition, we would have no soil problems; but when the products of a number of farms are required to artificially increase the fertility of one farm, where is the nation on an extended basis to get the manure necessary to bring back to life all the farms that exhaust themselves in an effort to help their feeble neighbor? Is he not foolish, who in order to strengthen one piece of land, is obliged to sap the strength of another? By such "farm-foolosophy" an endless chain of degeneracy is maintained not only at the expense of the soil health but also at the expense of the public health. The farmer must learn that in sickening the soil with manure and the parasites that flourish in corruption, he is contributing to the process of decay which is now eating at the heart of man.

The Bureau of Soils, United States Department of Agriculture, has done work for the nation of sufficient importance to send us back to the pyramids for wisdom. The politicians have not seen to it that the lessons have been applied.

Why should we talk of over-population or of insufficient food when we look at Japan, Germany, Italy, France and Spain? Japan, including the island of Formosa, embraces less than 150,000 square miles. In 1910 that little stretch of land supported over 51,000,000 people or 350 to the square mile. The United States with an area of more than 3,-600,000 square miles in the same year supported 93,000,000 people or 20 to the square mile. A significant ratio of 17 to 1!

The State of Texas alone contains 262,290 square miles and if populated like Japan could support all the people of the United States leaving all the other states with their abandoned cities and plains as birth places for a new race. If the United States were populated as thickly as Japan she could to-day support 1,265,789,400 people.

Why go to Japan for a contrast?

Germany with an area of a little more than two hundred thousand square miles supports 64,000,000 people, an average of 305 to the square mile. Italy with an area of 110,000 square miles supports a population of 33,500,000 an average of 304 to the square mile. France supports an average of 188 to the square mile; Portugal an average of 155 to the square mile.

Yet in the United States corn is dear because producing but 26 bushels to the acre there is not enough to go round. In Germany with her fertilizer of lava rock the farmer who does not produce 50 bushels per acre is ashamed.

We need not worry about over-population. We need not worry about bread famine. We need only worry about our failure to put our 10,000 little red school houses at the country cross-roads to a good use. We need only worry about the empty "isms" of our colleges and universities. We need only worry about continuous ignorance, denatured soil and denatured food.

CHAPTER XXVI.

FOOD REFORM IN THE GROCERY STORE—BULLETINS OF THE IDEAL GROCERY.

A man is as old as his arteries. The arteries harden through bad habits which retard the elimination of the blood, lymph, bone and tissue salts. Lime salts are deposited when by excesses we squander the phosphorus of our body and when by food follies we remove the phosphorus from our diet.

Right thinking, moderation in eating and drinking, proper exercise, honest food will regulate the hardening of the arteries. Excess eating, excess drinking, excess excitement, excess worry (all worry is excess) and excesses of all kinds make themselves felt first of all in the human heart.

The grocery stores of the future will consider the laws of the body and will do their share in promoting the happiness of the human heart. On their walls will appear some such signs as we will now set down.

CONDENSED MILK.

Our condensed milk contains the butter fats and other solids that ought to be there. A chain of grocery stores in New York City in 1911 paid a fine of $500.00 and the Department of Health seized and destroyed 40,000 cans of adulterated condensed milk. Condensed milk is a baby food. Draw your own conclusions.

JUSTICE.

The grocer who trifles knowingly, or through

lack of proper care, with the foods on which babies depend for their life should repent in jail.

LOOSE MILK.

We don't sell it. When nobody sells it more babies will survive.

VANILLA.

Our vanilla extract contains no tonka beans, coumarin or vanillin. It is made of vanilla beans and is not diluted. It is not sold in short weight decoy bottles.

SPICES.

We don't sell exhausted spices because the dentist needs oil of cloves, oil of cinnamon, etc. Our spices contain all the fixed and volatile oil nature put there.

FLAVORS.

We don't sell strawberry, raspberry, peach, banana, pineapple, pistachio, cherry extracts which are made from formic ether, oenanthic ether, valerianate ether, ethyl ether, amyl ether, benzoic ether, butyric ether, esters and aldehydes. This is a grocery store, not a drug store.

SPIRIT VINEGAR.

We don't sell it. Our cider vinegar comes from apples, not from acetic acid and coal-tar dye. Our wine vinegar comes from grapes. All vinegar is diluted with water. So is ours.

JAM.

A Society for the Prevention of Cruelty among Jams should be organized. Glucose, apple stock (skins and cores), apple juice (prepared from apple waste), inorganic phosphoric or tartaric acid, bold mention of "berries" on the neck strip of the jar with the sacred 1-10 of 1 per cent of benzoate of soda attached, give us the word "compound," also the shivers.

BLACKBALL.

If a store cannot OR WILL NOT tell the plain, blunt truth concerning every food product on its shelves, it is your privilege to stay out of that store.

TEA.

The Government's new Tea Test shows prussian blue, gypsum or other facing or coloring on doctored teas. NO DOCTORED TEAS HERE.

BUTTER.

Our butter is not "processed" butter or "renovated" butter. It has never seen a homogenizer. If you want a reworked mixture this is not the place.

OLEO.

We sell oleomargarine as such. It is all right but it is not butter. We would much rather eat it than a lot of some butter. It is pure.

FULL CREAM CHEESE.

We haven't any. Nobody has. There is no such thing. Our cheese is "whole milk" cheese. It contains all the cream the cow gave, but no more. "Skim milk" cheese is in the majority. Think it over.

MOLASSES.

All New Orleans molasses is bleached with sulphurous acid. The Supreme Court of Pennsylvania condemned sulphurous acid as a poison. Our molasses is darker than the bleached kind because it is not doped.

DRIED FRUITS.

We sell pure prunes, raisins, currants and citron. They are free from sulphurous acid. We sell sundried apples and apricots, but no other kind. If the public is satisfied with brunette raisins why does it want blonde peaches?

PURE MEANS NOTHING.

All eggs are "pure" eggs. The crab apple is just as "pure" as the greening. A piece of beef off the shin bone of an ox is just as pure as a porterhouse steak. The word "pure" is overpuffed with pride. It's quality that counts.

LEGAL.

If you want lime juice or any other food preserved with sulphurous acid it is legal. If you like such foods buy them, but not in the dark.

ECONOMY.

Small prunes contain twice as many pits and skins as large prunes. Which is cheaper, prune meat or prune pits? Think it over.

PURELY VEGETABLE.

"Purely vegetable" does not mean "harmless." Opium, strychnine, cocaine, laudenum are "purely vegetable."

ART.

We have no art department. Coal-tar dyes belong to the ribbon business, not the food business. "Harmless" color schemes are all right for the label, but not for the food.

CATSUP.

Our catsup is made from tomatoes, not from tomato pulp. It contains no potato starch or any other starch. It contains no coal-tar dye and is not preserved with benzoate.

ALUM.

The law allows alum in pickles, mince meat, relishes, baking powder. We don't. If you think alum is good for you just try it on your cat.

CANNED GOODS.

We don't buy last year's "jobs" or "overstocks" from the canner or packer to catch you with "bargain" prices. We sell no watered products. Add the water from your own spigot. Even if the Bureau of Water Supply does not give trading stamps, it is cheaper to get water from the spigot than the grocer.

JUGGLING.

All the jugglers are not in the circus. The same bag of coffee in this store is not dumped into three different bins to come out at three different prices.

HATS AND MUSHROOMS.

Panama hats are bleached with sulphurous acid. So are canned mushrooms and other things.

LACQUERED TINS.

If salts of tin were a good thing in your food God would have put them there, but he didn't. That's why we want all canned foods packed in lacquered tins or glass.

MINCE MEAT.

Our mince meat contains no "rejected" currants and raisins, no skins and cores and no filler of glucose. It contains no antiseptic. It was made for human beings, not for test tubes.

FRENCH FIZZLES.

We don't sell imported French peas, string beans, etc., colored with sulphate of copper. There is a law against them in Pennsylvania and another in this store.

GELATINE POWDERS.

Can't buy them here. The story is too miserable to be hung up in public places. Ask some one who knows. It will save us from bad talk.

CLEAN.

Our foods are covered. Sanitary protection means a little more to us than it does to some politically infested health departments.

NO FOOD FRAUD.

This is a pure food store. It won't tolerate any form of food fraud or deception. The drugs, dyes and flavors which politics have white-washed cannot get in here though they are legal. Politics and health laws don't go any better together than ice cream and beer.

BENZOATE.

If you want foods preserved with benzoate they sell them down the street. We won't sell them because we have no M. D. diploma that entitles us to prescribe medicine in a grocery store.

ONE DOSE.

One dose of the things we don't allow in our foods won't kill you. People don't die that way from food frauds. It is the bad history of food drugs and the bad things that food drugs conceal that we object to.

POLISHED RICE.

Polished rice won't do you as much harm as whiskey, but it won't do you the good that rice was designed to do when God made it his way. If the rice polisher knows more about what rice ought to be than the Almighty, where are his credentials?

OUR CAKES.

Our cakes contain eggs, not "egg color." If egg color was not a fraud intended to represent eggs that are off on a vacation, some other color would be used besides yellow and cakes would be lavender, purple, pink, green.

CORN MEAL.

We sell corn meal containing all of the corn, including the good part usually fed to hogs.

OAT MEAL.

Our oat meal contains all of the things that grew up in the oat. We don't believe any more in denaturing oats than we do in denaturing men and women.

WHOLE WHEAT BREAD.

Pale children often need foods, not drugs. Honest bread made from all of the wheat, nothing added and nothing taken away, will put life in the child.

BROWN RICE.

All natural rice is brown. That's the way it grows. You can make it white by denaturing it. What chance would a baby have if you denatured its milk?

WHITE FLOUR.

GOD put twelve vitalizing mineral salts into the wheat. MAN takes eight of them out in order to make flour white and then wonders why there are so many false teeth.

NATURAL LAWS.

You expect milk, eggs, meat, fish, tomatoes, etc., to spoil. Why? Because you know they will obey nature's laws. Don't expect other foods not to obey the same laws. They will unless you put "dope" in them.

CANDY.

Our candy contains no coal-tar dye, no flavoring ethers, no soap stone or radiator lacquer, no carpenter's glue, no paraffin, no shellac, no iron oxides, gum benzoin or substitute for pure chocolate.

FRESH EGGS.

Our eggs were not laid in Heaven. Every egg answers for its own career. We sell storage eggs under their right name. We sell near-by eggs for just what they are. All eggs are eggs. Fresh eggs are fresh eggs.

OUR BREAD.

Our bread is wrapped in sanitary wrappers. It is not pawed over by dirty fingers. Flies have to look elsewhere for a meal. Why have bread clean in the first place, if you don't keep it clean?

NATURE'S GIFTS.

Nature sends us hundreds of things out of life-giving earth. She intends us to eat them. Fresh lettuce, spinach, endives, celery, onions, carrots, parsnips, turnips, cauliflower, cabbage, etc. Nature wants us to eat oranges, lemons, grape fruit, apples, pineapple, figs, dates, bananas, plums, peaches, raspberries, strawberries, blackberries, currants, grapes, etc.

HAND-MADE.

The body must be built from building material. The body cannot get such material from the food unless it is in the food. Hand-made or artificial concoctions cannot stand beside nature's offerings. Thinks this over when you are hungry.

NUTS.

Walnuts, hickory nuts, peanuts, pecans, filberts, Brazils, almonds were made to eat. That's what we have teeth for.

GRAPE JUICE.

The juice of the grape comes from nature. It is one of the soft drinks we are glad to sell. Our other soft drinks are all right, too, because we don't have any. Grape juice does not need coal-tar dyes, ethereal flavors or benzoate.   Artificial concoctions do.

MEAT.

People forget that pea beans, marrow beans, red kidney beans, white kidney beans, black turtle beans, yellow eye beans, lima beans, green peas, yellow peas, white marrow peas, blackeye peas and lentils contain more protein or tissue-building material than roasts, steaks and chops.   People forget that the bean is beef, the pea is lamb, the lentil is pork.

WISDOM.

Wise is he who eats ripe fruit, matured greens and well cooked vegetables every day.

THE CHILD.

The conservation of the city boy and girl depends upon the honesty of its food.   We have printed suggestions for the child's breakfast, dinner and supper.   Take them home, study them, act upon them.   If everybody would do that we would come pretty close to having a nation of perfect men and women in twenty years.

CHAPTER XXVII.

AN IDEAL RESTAURANT.

Is the average American destined to perish miserably and immediately? He will not. He will travel along just as he travels now. His average of efficiency, buoyancy, good nature, endurance and vitality will be the same indifferent average that he finds everywhere around him. But he can improve his vigor and perhaps lengthen his life by being mindful of two things that he was not mindful of before.

In the first place, he must eat with an intelligent idea of the purpose of food. Food is not what one eats. Food is what one digests and assimilates. Keeping this idea in mind at meal times, let him make selection of the food he requires.

In the second place. instead of remaining indifferent to the gravity of modern food abuses, let him agitate reform and by slow but steady progress bring about a return to the honest and wholesome conditions under which living is at its best.

Let us consider a typical business man's luncheon at one of the city clubs or restaurants. It will be something like this:

Cocktail, oysters on the half shell, roast beef, mashed potatoes, asparagus, white bread, butter, pie, cheese, coffee.

There are a hundred variations of this luncheon but they are all quite similar in substance.

After eating the oysters and while waiting for his portion of beef, he nibbles upon white bread or rolls. He then eats all of the beef, as a rule quite hurriedly, a spoonful of mashed potatoes, the asparagus tips, all of the cheese and pie, and then while removing the band from his cigar, swallows his coffee.

Let us analyze that meal. The oyster while not essentially a food, but rather a condimental substance, contains, nevertheless, six per cent protein; the beef contains eighteen per cent protein; the cheese contains twenty-five per cent protein; the white bread contains nine per cent protein. At a low estimate nearly one-third of the business man's luncheon consists of protein food. He began the day with two eggs and a rasher of bacon. The eggs contain fifteen per cent protein, the bacon nine per cent. At his evening meal he will eat a big steak or its equivalent in chops and on top of this he consumes a generous portion of roquefort, camembert or some other similar cheese. Not only does his luncheon consist of excess protein, but the three meals of the day bring him about the same quantity.

He does not work in the ditch. His gentle exercise indoors rarely excites perspiration. He leads a sedentary life. Why does he eat so much protein? Does he not know that his organs of elimination are whipped to their utmost in order to dispose of the excess of nitrogen which such a diet imposes upon him.

On a diet of oats the horse travels all day, dragging an immense burden behind him. He is in action constantly. None of his organs of digestion have an opportunity to grow sluggish. But nature sees to it that his food contains only one-eighth or about twelve per cent of protein. The minerals are not removed.

The horse with its tremendous expenditure of physical energy requires twelve per cent protein. Man thinks he needs thirty-five per cent. As a result, man is a diligent reader of patent medicine advertisements. This does not mean that man should eat oats. It means that man should learn a lesson from the oat-eater.

He must realize that a diet overloaded with protein and minerally exhausted will not perform the same kind of service for him that a diet properly balanced in fat, protein, carbohydrates and organic mineral salts will render.

Some day a big hotel or a "Business Man's Lunch on Broadway" will throw its doors open to the public according to new principles. On the walls of the dining room statements like the following will appear:

We have prepared a dozen combination luncheons containing the foods to which you are most partial. You will find your favorite dishes represented in some one of these combinations. They have all been arranged on a well-balanced basis.

If split up and analyzed each of our combinations is approximately as follows:

Fat, four to eight per cent.

Protein, ten to fourteen per cent.

Carbohydrates, forty-five to sixty per cent.

Organic Mineral Salts, two to three per cent.

In cooking all our vegetables, legumes, greens, fruits and meats we carefully conserve the soluble salts. According to long recognized methods of cookery these valuable salts went down the waste pipe. The vegetables and greens in each combination afford the necessary bulk demanded by the peristaltic action of the digestive organs.

Booklets lying on each table will contain:

OUR STANDARDS.

MILK.

Pure clean milk contains the sixteen elements which the body requires for its growth and sustenance. Pure milk in addition to being a perfect food is also a perfect culture for the development of pathogenic (disease-breeding) bacteria. Therefore we use no "loose" milk. We serve "certified milk" only. This milk is produced under the direction of the County Medical Society, guaranteed absolutely free from disease-breeding bacteria.

Such milk is produced in sanitary dairies. The hands of the milkers are sterilized. The milkers themselves are under the supervision of examining physicians. When there is sickness in their homes they are not permitted to work. The cows are tested for tuberculosis. They are fed scientifically on balanced rations of whole grains and greens, grasses and the seeds of grasses. They are washed before milking.

The milk is cooled at once. All animal heat is withdrawn and at no time is the temperature allowed to rise above 45 degrees Fahrenheit. It is kept in sterilized bottles until served. At regular intervals, it undergoes a test for bacteria count. It is not skimmed. It contains all the butter fat produced by healthy cows, no more, no less.

Under such conditions pure milk of poor quality, milk contaminated with bacteria, milk from which the cream has been separated, milk to which water has been added, dirty milk, milk kept sweet by the action of chemical preservatives is impossible.

CREAM.

The value of cream is determined by its percentage of butter fat. Our cream must have the same pedigree as our milk. It must be clean, fresh and free from all micro-organisms except the beneficial lactic bacteria.

The difficulty of securing pure, fresh, wholesome cream with a sweet flavor, is not appreciated by the general public. We are mindful of that difficulty and no cream which falls below the National Standard for Butter Fat is tolerated by us.

ICE CREAM.

Our ice cream is made of a mixture of certified milk and cream and fresh eggs. It is flavored with pure vanilla, pure raspberries, pure strawberries, pure peaches, pure maple sap or pure filtered honey. It contains no commercial "binder" or "bodyfier." It contains no glucose. It contains no corn starch or other form of filler commonly employed in the production of commercial ice cream. The most delicate child may eat it with absolute freedom. Following is a recipe for making one of our frozen dainties which might be called "Milk and Honey of the Egyptians, Iced:"

One pint certified milk.

One pint pure cream (one quart certified milk may be used instead with delicious results).

Beat the yolks of two eggs.

Add 10 ounces pure filtered honey and beat again.

Beat the whites of two eggs stiff.

Add the beaten yolks and honey, mix thoroughly.

Add the milk, or cream and milk. Freeze.

For children, the milk, egg and honey mixture is more digestible than the mixture containing added cream. The most delicate child can eat it with impunity.

BUTTER.

Butter is made of many kinds. Most butter is a mere emulsion of artificially colored butter fat. It is colored with one of the permissible coal-tar dyes, annato or saffron. The peasants of Europe still appreciate the flavor of real butter. In the United States, butter flavor is almost forgotten. Most American butter makers separate the cream from the milk by a machine and the butter is churned at once, thus producing the emulsified mass with which most of us are familiar.

Butter to be worthy of the name must be produced from ripened cream which has undergone the normal lactic fermentation necessary to the development of butter flavor, also necessary for the destruction of any other organisms that may be present in the cream. We serve pure butter salted and unsalted. We tolerate no artificial color. The use of color is an imitation of butter made in June from cream which is the product of grass fed cows.

People do not demand that Swiss cheese shall be yellow, but for some capricious reason they want their butter to reach them under such a mask. Our standard represents a return to nature.

CHEESE.

Our cheese is uncolored for the same reason that our butter is uncolored. We do not serve "Full cream" cheese. Nobody does. There is no such thing. Cheese is either whole milk cheese containing all the fat the cow gave and no more, or skimmed milk cheese containing none of the fat the cow gave. Our cheese is the properly ripened whole milk product.

EGGS.

All eggs served in our Pure Food Restaurant must be not only fresh, but they must be produced by contented hens, properly fed on grains and greens. Our specifications for the production of eggs are just as rigid as our specifications for the production of milk. Storage eggs do not yield the inimitable flavor of fresh eggs produced by scientifically fed hens.

CHICKEN.

The ideal chicken, properly fed, develops small ·bones and a large plump breast. The Department of Agriculture has spent a great deal of time in teaching the poultry producer how to feed his chickens for health and vitality. Ground corn, wheat, barley, oats, grass, calcium carbonate and calcium phosphate, in the form of ground bone or oyster shells, together with necessary mineral salts to be found in healthy soil, constitute the food of all chickens served in our dining room. Storage chickens are taboo here. We make a specialty of a tender, meaty bird, roasted. The fine delicate flavor of our pure food chicken tells its own story better than we can.

TURKEY.

The only time to eat turkey is between Thanksgiving and last of March. Storage men will tell you that in spite of the large holiday consumption of turkeys, most turkeys are consumed between March and Thanksgiving, during the very period when they are out of season. Any chef who serves turkey during the summer is defying the laws of nature. In order to produce turkeys for summer consumption, the bird must be killed during the winter, frozen and kept in storage until called upon. The turkey should be consumed when it is fit. Freezing does not add to its flavor; on the contrary, physiological and chemical changes are set up during its long sleep on ice. The fine natural flavor of the bird is gradually lost and a new flavor sometimes extremely

objectionable, takes its place. In our Dining Room
we serve turkeys only when they are in season; that
is, when they are fit to eat; because of that fact we
do not have to resort to the storage man for our
supplies.

OYSTERS.

After taking the oyster from its bed, it is immersed in fresh water, under the influence of which
it becomes bloated and bleached producing an appearance of plumpness and firmness. The water in
which oysters are floated may not always be clean
water. Oysters take on whatever contamination
may be present in the water in which they are immersed. Oysters taken from infected beds are
frequently the cause of typhoid fever. The oysters
served in our Pure Food Restaurant are certified
oysters, procured from inspected beds which means
that they are absolutely free from bacteria.

GUINEA FOWLS.

September, October, November and December
are the only four months during which guinea fowls
should be consumed for the reason that during the
breeding season their fine flavor is distinctly marred.
In spite of this fact people do not ordinarily begin
to eat them until New Year day. In order to turn
the guinea fowl season topsy turvy, the bird has to
be killed, frozen, and put away until the misguided
connoisseur calls for it. There is no guinea fowl
on our menu only while it is in season and fit to eat.

SQUAB.

The common squab ordinarily served in the
average hotel or restaurant is known to the hotel
man as the "Banquet Squab." They cost from $1.75
to $2.50 per dozen. Like most other birds they are
educated through a long period of confinement in
ice before they are served. Such squabs by the art

of the average chef can be made to look delicious.
The brown and crackled parchment of the lately
frozen squab, delicately trimmed with fresh green
sprigs and served on immaculate china, is a sham.
We will have none of it. Squabs in season, fresh,
tender, wholesome, delicate, is our rule. No other
rule is recognized.

FISH.

The flesh of all fish is much less stable than the
flesh of meat-producing animals. It splits up more
rapidly than meat because the elements of which it
is composed are more loosely associated. Fish is
thus subject to the processes of decomposition at a
more rapid rate and with less resistance than meat.
Many intestinal troubles, including ptomaine pois-
oning, result from eating fish which is not strictly
fresh. For this reason no fish is served in our Pure
Food Restaurant out of season. The storage man's
influence is again kept at a distance. We will not
serve shad roe in winter. It is necessary to resort
to chemical preservatives or to embalming in ice
in order to carry the shad roe from its summer
origin into the winter's diet. So with all other fish.
Turkey in summer and shad roe in mid-winter are
details of a topsy turvy condition which we are
striving to set right.

MEATS.

We depend upon the Federal Inspection Service
of the United States Government for the integrity
of our meat supply, but exercise keen scrutiny in
selecting cuts of tender fibre. In cooking meats we
make a specialty of conserving the extractives containing the valuable tissue salts of phosphorus and
potassium. Boiled meats unless served in its own
juices is not a food, in fact dogs fed on meat which
previously has been subjected to the action of dis-

tilled water, thereby losing its tissue salts, will sicken and die. Roasted, broiled, stewed, curried or minced, we see to it that our meat dishes turn none of their valuable elements over to the soup pot. We have no method of utilizing by-products in our Restaurant.

SOUPS.

It is not possible to make good soups out of storage meat or fowl. The average hotel soup is a flavorless liquor colored with caramel, in which artistically chiselled vegetables and stars, crescents, circles, squares and letters of the alphabet made of Italian paste languidly float. Beef for the table should be ripened for nearly a month before eating, but beef for soup must be as fresh as possible. Soup properly made, contains the stimulating and vitalizing energy of the soluble salts contained in the vegetables, greens and meats used in its preparation. The French dietitian understands the real value of honest soup. Where we use grains, such as rice and barley, in making soup, we employ only the undenatured product, such as unpearled barley and unscoured and unpolished rice. These grains in their natural condition contain the iron, phosphorus, calcium manganese and other organic mineral compounds which nature elaborates in whole grains for man's benefit. We see to it that such grains reach our kitchens in their natural state.

VEGETABLES.

We serve two kinds of vegetables, fresh and canned, and give preference to such canned vegetables as are put up in lacquered tins or glass, thereby preventing the formation of salts of tin which are produced by the action of the vegetable acids on the metal base. The conduct of salts of tin in the human body is believed to exercise a pernicious influence on the kidneys and other organs. There are plenty of fresh vegetables to be obtained all the year round, although some people insist on winter vegetables in the summer and summer vegetables in the winter. Our bill of fare contains two vegetable headlines "Canned" and "Fresh." We serve no vegetables sweetened with saccharine or colored with sulphate of copper. In brief, our canned vegetables are absolutely free from coloring or any kind of preservative, or any kind of artificial flavoring, with the exception of common table salt.

FRUITS.

We serve fresh fruits and fruits preserved in cans and glass jars. The canned fruits must be packed in lacquered tins. The only method of preserving tolerated is by sterilizing with heat and by hermetical sealing. Benzoate of soda, fluoride of calcium and sulphurous acid, often employed in preserving fruits and vegetables, are not tolerated in our dining rooms, kitchen or pantry.

BREAD.

The elements removed from the natural grains in "refining" them to satisfy the artificial taste-standards of man, include the very substance of which the blood, bones, and tissues are constructed.

We serve two kinds of bread, the home made bread and honest whole wheat bread, containing all the wheat, nothing added and nothing removed.

Such bread has the rich, nutty, "wheatty" flavor of the whole grain.

Our Pure Food Restaurant is doing the city of —— a service of significant importance in restoring to its diet the certified loaf of whole wheat bread.

RICE.

Our rice puddings are made of natural, unscoured, unpolished rice, which contains all the elements which nature organized in the grain.

CORN MEAL.

Our corn bread, corn muffins and corn porridge are prepared from the certified whole corn-meal containing all of the corn.

EXTRACTS.

Our vanilla extract contains no Tonka beans, coumarin, vanillin or Tahiti beans. It is made of the Mexican Vanilla bean. Our lemon and orange extracts are prepared according to the United States Pharmacopoea standard. Fruit extracts made from formic ether, oenanthic ether, valerianate ether, butyric ether, benzoic ether, esters and aldehydes are barred. There is no law against them except in this restaurant.

SPICES.

Our spices contain all the fixed and volatile oil which nature put there. Our white pepper is the creamy white heart of the finest black pepper berry from which the outer shell, or wood fibre, is removed by a decorticating machine. You will note its fine creamy color and its splendid flavor. The color is due to nature. The leaden gray color of the average white pepper is the result of a bleaching process with lime.

CATSUP.

The law permits the use of coal tar dyes, benzoate of soda, tomato pulp, and artificial color in making catsup. We do not.

MINCE MEAT.

The law permits the use of the skins and cores of the canning factory and the rejected currants and raisins of the fruit jobber in making commercial mince meat. It also permits the use of aluminum sulphate, benzoate of soda and sulphurous acid in the mince meat. We do not. The package in which the chef receives the mince meat or any other chemically treated food, must be labelled under the law, but the chef is not obliged to label the pies or the dish containing the chemically treated food. This fact should be realized.

DRIED FRUITS.

We serve the finest dried prunes, raisins, currants and citron in our various dishes because they are dried by nature's methods. We do not serve dried peaches, pears, apricots or apples, because they are treated with sulphurous acid for a more sightly color, and they also take on 15% moisture which sells at fruit prices. Until these dried fruits go back to the old fashioned method, we will not serve them in our Pure Food Restaurant.

MOLASSES.

All New Orleans Molasses is bleached and preserved with sulphur dioxide. We will not use it. Instead we go to Barbadoes for our molasses, which is free from chemical treatment. It is darker than the New Orleans product, but it is pure and its flavor is delicious. Wherever we use molasses in cooking or baking we employ the Barbadoes molasses.

CONSERVES.

Jams and jellies for tarts, layer cakes, etc., and the jellies served with meats are prepared for restaurant use from glucose, apple-stock, apple juice, prepared from apple waste, phosphoric acid or tartaric acid with benzoate of soda. The package when it reaches the chef is always marked "compound," and bears a label indicating the presence of the artificial color and chemical preservative employed. This

secret knowledge never filters out into the dining
room.

We employ no compound jams or jellies. Our
jams are made, pound for pound, of fresh fruit and
such sugar as we can get. We use no canned stock
or barrel stock. Our jellies are made from the
freshly expressed juice of fresh ripe fruit and sugar.

GELATINE POWDERS.

We do not employ Jelly Powder in the preparation of our foods. Gelatine is not a food. It is an
artificial product prepared by chemical treatment
from the bones, sinews and hides of animals. When
finished it has no color, no flavor and no odor. All
these accidents are conferred upon gelatine by chemical processes. We admit that gelatine dishes look
nice, but food is not a matter of nicety. Anything
bordering on sham is kept out of our dining rooms
on principle.

MARASCHINO CHERRIES.

Maraschino cherries are first bleached with sulphurous acid to remove the freckles. They are then
dyed with aniline like a feather or a ribbon and
then preserved with benzoate. For this reason we
do not use maraschino cherries.

CAKES.

Our cakes contain no "egg color."

BAKING POWDER.

It is legal to use calcium acid phosphate and
aluminum sulphate in the manufacture of baking
powder. We prefer cream of tartar baking powder
and stick to it.

OLIVE OIL.

The absence of free fatty acid is the test by which
the quality of olive oil is determined. If the oil is
pressed from olives gathered from the ground

bruised olives, or if some of the olives are beginning
to decay, the oil produced from such olives will contain free fatty acid and the presence or absence of
free fatty acid is the absolute indicator of the character of olives employed in the production of the oil.

Fully matured hand-selected olives, properly
pressed and properly safe-guarded from contamination will produce oil which emerges from the chemical test with a perfect pedigree. Our olive oil must
not only defy the chemical test for free fatty acid,
but it must also resist the test for cotton seed oil.

MAPLE SYRUP.

We serve no mixture of cane sugar and maple
sugar. The so-called pancake syrup used in restaurants and hotels, contains 85% cane syrup and 15%
maple syrup. Our maple syrup is the pure sap of
the maple tree, boiled in open kettles to the consistency of syrup; nothing is added in the form of
chemical preservatives, filler or dilution of any
kind whatsoever.

These brief outlines indicate the extraordinarily
high ideals which we have set out to realize in the
conduct of this Pure Food Restaurant

It will discriminate not only in purity but in
quality.

A food may be pure and still be scarcely fit to eat.
A piece of shin meat from the leg of an ox is just as
pure as a porterhouse steak. A crab apple is just as
pure as a greening or a northern spy.

Pure and good are two words which in the food
world should never be separated. In our Pure Food
Restaurant, it is our purpose always to unite them
and keep them together.

Where in the United States or Europe is there
another eating house modeled on such lines?

COPYRIGHT. 1912. BY THE COMMERCIAL ADVERTISER ASS'N. ONE CENT.

SECRETS OF FOOD ADULTERATION BY BAKERS REVEALED

How Two "Innocent Grocers" From Carbondale, Pa., Went to the Show at the Garden and Asked a Few Questions—How the Answers Came Promptly Concerning the Use of Queer Matter in Cooking.

ANCIENT EGGS AVAILABLE IN MORE WAYS THAN ONE

Demonstrators at Public Exhibition Explain the Mysteries of What Is Just as Good as Butter—Also Fancy "Icing" for Cakes and the Use of Alcohol—Light on the Meaning of That Label "Guaranteed Under the Pure Food and Drugs Act."

Heading in the N. Y. Globe of the expose of the Bakers' and Confectioners' methods.

CHAPTER XXVIII.

STARTING A BAKERY.

New York bakers are selling their customers pies and cakes containing benzoate of soda and artificial colorings. They are using dried eggs—in many instances "rots and spots"—artificial flavorings, and their pie and cake fillings are made up of fresh and dried fruits that have become so spoiled that they are unsalable.

Almost anything is good enough to go into a baker's pie. Spoiled canned goods, called "swell heads," because fermentation bulges out the cans, make excellent fillings for pies, and there is no use in paying regular rates for good raisins when you can wash out mouldy and wormy ones and nobody ever will know the difference.

All this and more was told in confidence by agents of bakers' supply houses to a reporter for The Globe who visited the Baking and Candy Show at Madison Square Garden, New York, with Alfred W. McCann, a pure food expert and member of the vigilance committee both of the national and local advertising clubs.

Mr. McCann and The Globe reporter went as grocers from Carbondale, Pa., who knew nothing about the baking business, but thought it would be a good department to add to the grocery business.

Eagerly the salesmen in the different booths at the Bakers' Show dilated upon the profits of the busi-

ness. All were agreed that no baker ever used many
pure products in his goods.

"There isn't a baker in the United States," said
one man, "who isn't using goods that contain 'benzo.'"

"Benzo" is the popular contraction for benzoate
of soda, the preservative against which Dr. Harvey
W. Wiley has waged such relentless war.

"I understand," Mr. McCann said, "that we can
use all our spoiled fruits in making pies, that we
won't need to throw away unsalable stuff."

"Certainly," said the salesman. "All you have to
do is to wash them out a little and boil them up and
they are all right."

"Do you mean that any kind of spoiled fruit is
good enough for pies?" the reporter asked.

"Almost any kind," the salesman answered.
"Most bakers go over the bad fruit and pick out
some that is too far gone, of course, but the majority of your unsalable stuff will do for pies."

The salesman showed a bottle of "butter flavoring" that looked like partly refined petroleum. "No
baker ever uses butter in his cooking," he said. "All
you need to do to make twelve pounds of cooking
butter is to take a dollar's worth of lard compound,
not pure lard, and mix it with half a cent's worth
of 'butter flavor.' Then you have twelve pounds of
cooking butter."

He also had a powder out of which cream puff
filler was made. If you make your own you have to
use eggs which cost, the salesman said, 25 cents a
dozen now. These are low grade eggs. The powder
is made of dried eggs that cost far less than 25 cents
a dozen.

Then you can buy icing for cakes, all ready to be
mixed with sugar and water. There is orange icing

of a deep red; chocolate, nearly black. These colors are made deep so that a little will go a long way. The bakers know that when a person eats a cake that looks like chocolate he will think he is eating a chocolate cake. Just a touch of flavoring is all that is necessary. Gloss and color are most necessary.

"What about the pure food laws?" asked Mr. McCann. "They're pretty strict in Carbondale."

"No need to worry," said the salesman. "We label everything that is artificially colored or that contains preservatives. Everything we have is guaranteed under the pure food laws."

"Guaranteed?"

"That means that it complies with the law—it's labelled imitation, you know."

"The law doesn't guarantee anything, does it?"

"Oh, no, but the word sounds good."

"But will we have to label our pies and cakes when we put benzoate of soda and artificial colorings in them?"

"Certainly not. You don't need to worry about the pure food law. We label all our stuff."

"Then you don't have to inform the consumer that you are using benzoate of soda and artificial colorings?" Mr. McCann asked.

"Certainly not. The stuff is marked in the original packages, that's all that's necessary. You don't have to hang up any sign telling the people what's in your pies. You know what's in them. That's all the law demands."

The reporter said it certainly was, and inquired whether spoiled pumpkins could be put into pies without fear of detection.

The salesman admitted it was done often, but the spoiled fruits were generally used.

The salesman said there was no way in which a 10-cent pie could be made to cost more than 3½ cents.

There were on exhibit buckets of mince meat, imitation eggs, imitation cream, imitation baking powder, cake filling, all kinds of pie filling, and imitation flavoring extracts.

Here you could buy mincemeat at 9 cents a pound, add 100% water or cider, and cut it to 4½ cents a pound, according to a salesman. This is all ready to be put into the pies, so is the pie filling, which comes in all flavors. It never spoils, the salesman said, and it is labelled with the benzoate of soda label. Of course the customer doesn't know he is eating "benzo." Unless he goes into the back room of the bakery and looks at the kegs, he is likely to think he is buying fresh fruit pies.

"We had a little scare in New York a year or so ago," said the salesman, "and some of the bakers were scared and began hanging up signs and cleaning up, but it all blew over. If you are afraid of the inspectors you can hang up a little sign saying that some of your goods are artificially preserved. It doesn't mean anything to your customers and complies with the law."

The salesman admitted that all his goods were preserved with "benzo." "You've got to do it," he said. "I know one fellow who gets around it by doctoring his stuff with grain alcohol, the stuff they rub on you in a Turkish bath. Think of putting that stuff in your stomach."

Over in the corner were soda fountain syrups and fruits beautifully colored. You could buy a powder which would keep ice cream from melting unless exposed to heat over 72 degrees.

Down the aisle were candies, the penny kind, meant for children, painted in all sorts of colors.

"It would be better for the children to eat the heads of their painted wooden soldiers," said Mr. McCann, "than to eat that stuff."

THE NEXT DAY.

The next day after the dealers in bakers' supplies had read the story in the Globe, they were up in arms, denouncing as "malicious lies" the statements in the Globe of how spoiled fruits were used, embalmed with benzoate of soda and colored with coal tar dyes. So once more the reporter visited the plant. When pinned down to point out exact statements that are false, the manufacturers practically admitted their truth, but complained that the "tone" was hostile—and added that there was no use of stirring up things and worrying the public. "Besides," they said, "benzoate of soda and coal tar dyes never hurt anybody."

However, the manufacturers of goods that are not artificially preserved and colored take great care to announce that fact, while the manufacturers who do use benzoate of soda and artificial colors do their best to conceal the fact. Firms using benzoate of soda cannot do business in Indiana or Florida, as the use of that drug as a preservative is prohibited in those states. The members of one firm objected to the reporter's use of the word "imitation." Those things were "compounds," not "imitations," they said. The reporter pointed to a can of Creamaline. "That is not imitation cream," said the dealer, "that is a 'bodifier'." The salesmen generally repudiated or denied the statements of the day before. The dealer at last exclaimed, "Nowadays the bakers are frightened to death if you say benzoate of soda. It is all because such men as you,

McCann, have stirred them up. You are a public nuisance. I believe the state law is unconstitutional. If you will start in business, as you pretended you were going to do, and get arrested for selling our goods, we will defend you and beat the benzoate question."

"I'll do it," said Mr. McCann. "If you won, it would be the greatest advertisement you could ask for. If you'll stand by that statement, I'll be the subject for a test case as soon as you like."

Another member of the firm backed down. "We wouldn't defend you, but we'll defend any of our regular customers who get into trouble by selling our goods."

The president of the State Association of Master Bakers came forward with a denial that they used spoiled goods or benzoate of soda preservative in their pies.

Another dealer demanded to be shown the clerk who told how to use spoiled fruits in pies. "If we pointed him out," the reporter asked, "would you discharge him?"

"I don't know what I would do," was the answer. "But your article is a pack of lies."

Another dealer said hotly, "Why didn't you say you were a reporter instead of sneaking round and posing as a grocer?"

"Then," said the reporter, as he turned to go, "you don't make the same statements to newspaper men that you do to prospective customers?"

AN INTERVIEW WITH DR. WILEY.

The greatest of the battlers in the cause of pure food, Dr. Harvey W. Wiley, sees victory ahead for the cause. He believes that when Woodrow Wilson becomes president the food adulterators and misbranders will be put to rout.

"What do you expect the new administration to do in the way of aiding the pure food cause?" he was asked by a Globe reporter.

"It is my hope," he answered, "that all the restrictions and gags that have been in force throughout the last two administrations will be removed, and that the law will be allowed to take its course, as intended by Congress.

"I hope that violators of the pure food laws will be taken to court and punished, and that there will be no more boards and referees to act as a buffer between the food manufacturer and the law."

"The Remsen board was dealt a crushing blow by Justice Anderson in the suit against the state of Indiana to force it to permit the sale of products preserved with benzoate of soda. Justice Anderson said the board didn't have one iota of evidence that benzoate of soda was harmless, and the suit was dismissed.

"I hope Mr. Wilson will restore the authority taken from the Bureau of Chemistry and give the officials a chance to enforce the law in the way Congress intended it should be enforced.

"The present state of affairs is the greatest disgrace ever attached to a free people, and the existence of these conditions is due solely to the fact that officials are protecting the criminals who sell misbranded and adulterated food. This stuff loaded with glucose and benzoate of soda is not fit to feed to fishes."

"How did the food manufacturers get such power?" Dr. Wiley was asked.

"The same way all big industries get power."

"Do you know of any instances of where food manufacturers contributed to campaign funds?"

"If they didn't contribute they should have, for they have made millions of dollars by feeding these concoctions to the people."

"Such conditions as were shown by the exposure at the Baking and Candy Show could not exist," Dr. Wiley said, "if the high officials were not corrupt."

J S ABBOTT, COMMISSIONER
CHEMIST AND BACTERIOLOGIST
MISS KATE CASPARIS,
SECRETARY
R H HOFFMAN, JR
ASSISTANT CHEMIST
E. H. GOLAZ
ASSISTANT CHEMIST

Food and Drug Department
State of Texas
Austin

P B. TILSON, HOUSTON
COLLABORATING CHEMIST
U S DEPARTMENT OF AGRICULTURE
H ANTHONY,
INSPECTOR
TOM H. JOHNSON,
INSPECTOR

Nov. 15, 1912.

Mr. Alfred W. McCann,

    c/o The Globe,

      New York, N. Y.

Dear Sir:

      I wish to congratulate you on the exposure of indecent methods in the bakery business. From such a suggestion, this department will investigate the whole bakery business in Texas.

                Yours truly,

                        FOOD AND DRUG COMMISSIONER.

JSA

CHAPTER XXIX.

FOR PHYSICIANS ONLY.

This chapter presents facts concerning the principal sixteen elements found in natural food, and in the body of man, which every physician should know at once. With these facts before him, he will realize that the present food situation is murderous and his medical associations will demand reform, as soon as the individual begins to appreciate the monstrous character of the food manufacturer's defiance of the very laws with which the physician is so much concerned.

While this chapter is not written for the lay-reader, and can be passed over without losing the meaning of any of the other chapters, it would be well for her who is approaching that most sacred experience of womanhood, to read it again and again, for after all, the conditions which these pages uncover, center around this chapter.

The organized club women of America could do no better thing than to begin a crusade, with this chapter as its foundation.

Following is a description of the sixteen elements of which the human body is composed. Taken singly, the average man and woman is familiar with them all, and sees and understands their use in the commonplace circumstances of life. Apparently it is only when they are assembled, that their technical names awe the understanding, and make them appear hopelessly mysterious. They are in reality very simple, and when briefly described, all the difficulties usually associated with them quickly melt away. So, we will take them one by one, and learn their offices as familiar and intimate friends, working constantly, day and night, asleep or awake, for our good. The great thing that we must know about them, is how to safeguard them from unfriendly hands.

POTASSIUM.

Potassium is found most abundantly in the soft solid tissues, in the corpuscles of the blood, the muscle protoplasm, and in the fluids secreted by some of the glandular organs such as milk. Whereas sodiums occurs chiefly in the form of chloride in the blood and other fluids, potassium occurs chiefly as phosphate in the cells. This indicates that the cells pick and choose in obedience to a fixed law, and select such elements as are necessary to their normal life and functioning. This selective action is inhibited if the cells cannot find the material to be selected. How can they find it when it is largely or totally removed from food? Without the potassium and other salts normal osmotic pressure could not be maintained in the tissues, and the body fluids in which the organs are bathed would lack their characteristic influence upon the elasticity and irritability of muscle and nerve. Moreover, the acid and alkaline digestive juices and other secretions could not find the bases on which they are formed, and the internal fluids could not maintain the neutrality or slight alkalescence necessary to body equilibrium. Potassium and sodium antagonize and balance the calcium in tissues and fluids. The alternate contractions and relaxations of the heart movement depend upon the potassium, sodium and calcium in the fluid which bathes the heart muscle.

What food industry has the right to interfere with
the presence of these salts which nature so wonderfully prepares in the normal food of animal and
man?

If nature does not set the proper standard why
is it that man's artificial attempt to change nature's
formula always results in disaster to the animal
fed upon his juggled product?   Every dietetic experiment ever undertaken proves this.

Potassium is a mineral so widely distributed in
nature that no animal or edible plant has life or
can have life without it.

Notwithstanding its generous diffusion over the
whole earth, it never occurs uncombined, or in a
free state.   It is found in many combinations with
both organic and inorganic acids, but never pure.
There is no such thing as pure potassium outside
the chemical laboratory, just as there is no such
thing as pure sugar or starch in nature.

When separated by the skill of the chemist from
any of its many combined states, it is silvery-white
in color, has a decided metallic lustre, and becomes,
like pure arsenic, a deadly agent of destruction.

There is only one metal, lithium, which is lighter
in weight.   At ordinary temperature, it is soft
enough to be cut with ease with a table knife, but
at the freezing point of water, it is quite brittle,
and breaks into crystals.

In perfectly pure dry air, it undergoes no
change, but in ordinary air it quickly unites with
hydrogen and carbon, and becomes coated with a
film of potassium hydrate and carbonate.

It has such a greedy and insatiable affinity for
water, that when the two are brought together a
wonderful phenomenon is immediately observed.
The potassium undergoes almost instantaneous de-

composition, and sputters and hisses over the surface of the water on which it floats with such liberation of energy that great heat evolves. This heat is sufficient to set fire to the escaping hydrogen, which bursts into a beautiful lilac flame.

With two single exceptions, caesium and rubidium, potassium is the most electropositive element in nature. It will doubtless be proved before many years that its electrolytical influence on the human body is one of the most vital processes of life.

The layman is familiar with potassium in many forms, yet feels that it is too big for him to grapple with, and in consequence makes no effort to appreciate its importance in his diet. He knows that chloride of potassium is used in fertilizing the soil; that chlorate of potassium is used in the manufacture of explosives; that nitrate of potassium is used in medicine; that carbonate of potassium is used in making soap and glass; that cyanide of potassium, a violent poison, is used in photography. These things present no difficulty to his understanding, but for some strange reason he remains indifferent to the necessity of potassium in his food.

Potassium in several forms is absolutely necessary to life, and yet in its pure state it would destroy life. Nature for this reason abhors pure potassium, and will not tolerate it, except under artificial circumstances. That food factories have a right to remove the potassium salts from the food of man, is one of the many evidences of our national ignorance in the presence of life and death.

PHOSPHORUS.

Without the phosphorus compounds, there would be no living cell in the body. Sherman makes this statement: "Possibly because the crudity of the views formerly held and still sometimes met (especially in fraudulent advertisements of proprietary foods) tended to bring the subject into ridicule, the study of the phosphates, and other phosphorus compounds in food and nutrition was very generally neglected. Recently, however, the significance of phsophorus in the growth, development and functions of the organism is at last being adequately recognized."

The investigations of Forbes, Ohio Experiment Station, and Hart, Wisconsin Experimeutal Station, indicate that much of the mal-nutrition is not due to a low protein diet, but to a deficiency of phosphorus and calcium in the food.

Phosphorus is found in the body as phosphorized proteins called nucleo-proteins existing in the cells and tissues. True phospho-proteins exist in casein and ovovitellin. In brain and nerve substances and also to some extent in other tissues, the phosphorus appears as phosphorized fats termed lecithins. Egg yolk is particularly rich in this form of phosphorus, so are whole grains and legumes. Less highly organized forms of phosphorus are utilized by the body as phytin compounds, or phytates. Wheat, corn, rice, barley, and oats, in their natural unrefined state contain phosphorus in this form in abundant quantities. In the fluids and soft tissues of the body, the phosphorus is found in an inorganic form as potassium phosphate. In the bone structure, the phosphorus is found as calcium phosphate. Maxwell, in observing germinating seeds, and developing chic embryos, found that in the construction of the tissues of the growing vegetable or animal organism, the phosphorized fats played a most important part. Steinitz, Zadik, and Leipziger, discovered that these various phosphorus compounds could not be substituted for each other.

Simple proteins with inorganic phosphates, do not make a substitute for phospho-proteins. Rohmann showed that the phosphorized proteins furnished the material for tissue growth. Gumpert and Ehrstom found that phosphorus equilibrium was maintained in experiments upon men, when consumed in the form of phospho-proteins, casein, whereas, when taken as dicalcium phosphate or as the potassium phosphate of meat, the same quantity of phosphorus would not serve the needs of the body.

The phosphorus of wheat bran occurs chiefly in the form of phytates. These phytates are easily extracted, and readily absorbed in the digestive tract. When bran is leached in distilled water, the phosphorus is extracted. Such bran fed to cows, produces constipation, exploding the old time theory that the intestines were "scoured" by the coarse particles of bran, thus promoting peristalsis. Not the coarse particles, but the phosphorus contained in them is responsible for the gentle laxative effects produced by the bran.

The modern wheat miller, who produces refined patent flour, points to the statements of several chemists, indicating that refined patent flour is a more wholesome product for babes and invalids, than the meal made from the whole grain.

The writer has proved the folly of these statements on his own and other children.

Even when fasting, the phosphorus compounds of the body are broken down, and eliminated, showing the absurdity of removing these phosphorus compounds by mechanical processes from our foods. They are needed in the functioning of all the organs, and when not present, the bones and tissues, yes, the blood itself, are called upon to supply the deficiency.

The wheat, barley and corn mills of the West, the rice and corn mills of the South and Southwest, and the refined sugar and glucose industries producing their degerminated, dephosphorized, refined products, go hand in hand with malnutrition to the untimely graves of America.

The modern baked bean as usually sold in cans, is devitalized by the absurd processes through which it goes, in a thoughtless effort of the food manufacturer to rob it of its phosphorus. The beans are soaked over night in cold water. The excess water containing valuable solubles is then thrown off. The beans are then put in copper kettles, and boiled for 30 minutes. The phosphorized proteins rise to the top as a "scum" which is skimmed off, and poured into the sewer. The beans are then drained, and the chef stands idly by, while their rich vitality is poured down the waste pipe. The denatured product is then put into cans, sealed and cooked in a sterilizer for two hours, after which the so-called "baked" bean robbed of its phosphorus is put on the market.

Hart, in feeding hogs, in experiments conducted in the Wisconsin experiment station, found that 1.12 grams of phosphorus per day, was just about sufficient for the hogs; until they attained a weight of about 85 pounds, after which this quantity was clearly insufficient for the needs of the animal.

Sherman makes this statment: "1.12 grams phosphorus, would hardly seem a desirable amount for a growing child of the same size, or for a fully grown man or woman."

Sherman, Mettler and Sinclair, in bulletin 227, Office of Experiment Stations, United States Department of Agriculture, report a comparison of the amount of phosphorus contained in the food of typical American families, showing that a freely chosen diet of our denatured food products, does not furnish much more than 1.12 grams of phosphorus estimated as 2.75 grams, P_2O_5. These investigations were carried out in 20 American dietaries, including a lawyer's family in Pittsburg, a teacher's family in Indiana, a school superintendent's family in Chicago, a teacher's family in New York, a student's club in Tennessee, 115 women students in Ohio, a carpet dyer's family in New York, a sewing woman's family in New York, a house decorator's family in Pittsburg, a glass blower's family in Pittsburg, two mill workers' families in Pittsburg, a mechanic's family in Knoxville, Tenn., 30 lumber men in Maine, a farmer's family in Connecticut, a farmer's and mechanic's family in Tennessee, 13 men students, 5 women students, and one child in Knoxville, Tenn., boarding house, two negro farmers' families in Alabama.

The study continued 58 days, and took the average from 12,238 meals taken by men, and 793 meals taken by women. Speaking of these experiments, Sherman declares: "These results indicate that present food habits lead to a deficiency of phosphorus compounds, and it is not improbable that many cases of malnutrition are really due to an inadequate supply of phosphorus compounds."

Phosphorus like potassium is not found in nature in a free state, but is always combined with some other substance, such as oxygen, calcium and magnesium. No form of animal or vegetable life can be found, in which phosphorus does not play an indispensable part.

When artificially purified, it is semi-transparent and colorless. At ordinary temperature it is soft and easily cut. By the aid of heat, it is soluble in

fixed and volatile oils, and is exceedingly inflam-
able. At ordinary temperature it undergoes slow
combustion, emitting a peculiar white vapor, which
is luminous in the dark and which possesses an odor
quite similar to garlic. The slightest degree of heat
is sufficient to set it on fire. In fact, it is so subtle,
that gentle pressure between the fingers or slight
friction of any kind kindles it readily.

When set on fire, it burns rapidly, emitting a
beautiful white light and intense heat. In pure
oxygen its combustion is very rapid, and its light
far more vivid. The perfect combustion of phosphorus forms another substance, which is called
phosphorus pentoxid, a white solid that readily
takes up water, thus becoming phosphoric acid.
This is a colorless, odorless syrup with an intensely
sour taste, and is used by jam and jelly makers with
the permission of the law, although it is a deadly
poison. It is also used in the manufacture of soft
drinks. Phosphorus in this form is not the phosphorus required by the human or animal body.
Its use is criminal and must be stopped.

The fumes of phosphorus cause necrosis of the
bones, and are responsible for the dread disease
known as "phossy jaw" among the workers in the
phosphorus match factories.

Mixed with a paste, it is used for the destruction of vermin, rats, mice, cockroaches, etc., which
it quickly poisons. In its properly combined and
natural states, as found in the food of man, it is
one of the most necessary elements. Like the salts
of potassium, it is largely removed by the food
manufacturer from much of our diet, particularly
from our bread, bread stuffs, cereals and patent
foods of the refined type.

CALCIUM.

The most striking function of the salts of calcium in the body is observed in their effect upon the coagulation of the blood, and the contractility of the muscular tissue of the heart. An artificial solution of blood "ash," containing the small but necessary percentage of calcium, potassium and sodium will keep a heart beating normally for a long time, after it has been removed from the body of the animal. If the sodium and potassium are removed from the solution, the calcium will cause a condition of tonic contraction. If the calcium is removed, the sodium and potassium cause the heart muscle to relax. When present together in proper proportions, the muscle relaxes, and contracts in rythmical order. Meltzer states: "Calcium is capable of correcting the disturbances of the inorganic equilibrium in the animal body, whatever the deviations from the normal may be. Any abnormal effect which sodium, potassium or magnesium may produce in the direction of increased or decreased irritability, calcium is capable of re-establishing the normal equilibrim."

When fasting, calcium salts are lost through the intestinal wall proving that the body must have a constantly renewed supply of the mineral for its normal life processes.

As the bones and teeth make good the loss of calcium from the soft tissues and blood when no food is taken at all so do they also make good the loss when food deficient in calcium is consumed.

The injurious results that follow a calcium free diet is more pronounced on growing animals than on those full-grown. Ninety-nine per cent of the calcium appropriated by the growing animal goes to its bones and teeth. An abundance of calcium for the growing bones is thus an evident need. In its mother's womb, the growing child derives its calcium from the mother's food, provided the calcium has not been removed from her food. When that happens, as it always does on a diet consisting largely of white bread, polished rice, modern corn meal, glucose and sugar, the mother's bones and teeth are called upon to make up the deficiency. This deficiency, with the appalling results on the future health of the mother, is entirely preventable and uncalled for. Natural food makes such deficiency impossible. White bread, biscuits, crackers, cakes and all other forms of denatured grains and sugars kill mother and child before their time, or so rob them of normal vitality as to make their lives burdensome, inefficient and miserable.

Men who serve as subjects of calcium experiments do not need as much calcium as growing children. Any attempt to establish the minimum calcium requirement of the growing child from experiments made on adults will result disastrously to the child. Refined sugar and glucose are calcium free and calcium-hungry. They not only do not supply calcium to the body, but they take it from the body. Prescribe foods robbed of their calcium to the child, and in addition recommend the generous use of refined sugars and candy in the child's diet, and our 15,000,000 physically defective school children will become 10,000,000 physically defective men and women, and 5,000,000 of them will never become men and women at all.

Undenatured grains, parsnips, carrots, turnips, egg yolk and pure milk with plenty of greens, (in their own juice if cooked and the same applies to the vegetables mentioned) provide the richest calcium foods. Those who are to become mothers should know this if they would escape the disorders now generally looked upon as inevitable with child birth.

Calcium is a metal having a light yellow color, and a brilliant lustre. It is about as hard as gold. It oxidizes readily in moist air, and at a red heat burns vividly, forming quick lime. In combination with water, the quick lime forms slaked lime.

Like potassium and phosphorus, it is never found in nature in its pure state, but always in compounds widely distributed. Marble and chalk are simply calcium carbonate. Gypsum is simply calcium sulphate. The calcium light of the theatre is produced by turning a stream of oxygen and a stream of hydrogen in a state of ignition upon a lump of calcium.

Most people are perfectly familiar with its uses outside their own bodies, but do not realize that without calcium there can be no vegetable or animal life. "Rickets" is simply deranged or impaired calcium metabolism.

The food manufacturer does not know that he is committing a sin against nature and a crime against the race when he removes the calcium from our food.

IRON.

The inorganic iron of some drinking water and the inorganic medicinal iron prescribed to the anemic do not replace the complex organic iron compounds of greens, egg yolk, whole grains, or vegetables.

Socin fed two groups of mice, giving food to one group free from iron, plus medicinal iron in the form of inorganic iron chloride. To the other group, he gave the same iron-free food plus the addition

of egg yolk containing the iron in a highly organized form.

All of the mice on the artificial iron diet were
dead before the thirty-third day of the experiment.

The other mice fed with iron as prepared by
nature, not only lived, but gained in weight.

Lelensky fed dogs upon polished rice, from
which the iron compounds are removed, in order
to determine the effect of such iron-free diet upon
the hemoglobin content of the blood. In one dog,
the percentage of hemoglobin fell in nine days from
18.5 to 13.1; in another from 14.8 to 11.3 in six
days. The anemia became more pronounced as the
polished rice diet was continued, and on the eighteenth day, the dog died, yet the rice millers of the
United States are now circulating literature among
the grocers of the country denouncing the "fanatic-
ism" of those who urge the use of rice as nature
prepares it. These millers say in their circular:
"The people of the United States, in eating rice, by
the addition of a little gravy or butter more than
replace the protein and fat removed from the grain
by milling."

They persist in fogging the situation by refer-
ring to "protein" and "fat" as the missing links, and
do not show that "gravy" or "butter" supplies the
organic iron, phosphorus and other priceless mineral compounds of the whole grain. Dogs and children will die just as quickly on a diet of polished
rice with butter and gravy as on a diet of plain
polished rice. On a diet of natural rice they will
thrive.

It has been established that the iron demanded
by the body-processes of oxydation, secretion,, re-
production and growth must be obtained from food-
iron, not from medicine or mineral salts. The wan-

ton removal of this food-iron from our cereals, wheat, corn, rice, barley, sugar and glucose, by refining processes, and the loss of much of our vegetable iron by ignorant home cooking cannot be justified by any food industry, however great its investments in dollars and cents. The national health is of greater value than all the gold of the world.

Henry C. Sherman, Columbia University, shows the iron content estimated in milligrams per 100 grams of whole wheat as 5.2. The same figures for white, denatured, patent flour are 1.5, a tragic loss that no ""gravy" or "butter" can ever replace in the bodies of our anemic women and children.

Because fruits and vegetables contain a high water content, and low proportions of protein and fat, some dietitians hold them in low regard, forgetting that they are important sources of food-iron. Because the small traces of iron in meat have a distinctly lower value than the iron compounds of eggs, whole grains, vegetables and fruits, Van Norden points the folly of relying upon meat as a source of iron for young children. He advocates a liberal use of meat in the diet of the adult, but no meat for the child. He says: "As far as our children are concerned, we believe we could do better by following the diet of the most rigid vegetarians than by feeding the children as though they were carnivora, according to the bad custom which still prevails. If we limit the child's supply of fruit and vegetable iron we cause a certain sluggishness of blood formation and an entire lack of reserve iron, such as is normally found in the liver, spleen and bone marrow of healthy, well-nourished individuals."

Sherman reports an experimental dietary study made in New York City in which it was found that a free use of fresh vegetables, whole wheat bread, and the cheaper sorts of fruits, with milk but without meat, resulted in a gain of 30 per cent in the iron content of the diet, while the protein fuel value, and cost remained practically the same as in the ordinary mixed diet obtained under the same market conditions. The writer's children, with the exception of chicken once a month, have never eaten meat or asked for it, although the adult members of his family eat it twice a week.

Herbivorous animals get more iron in their diet than meat-eating animals, and not only live longer, but according to Sherman, are also less liable to anemia. It must be noted that these grass and grain eating animals get all the iron of their diet, whereas the human animal not only loses the greater part of it in his refined wheat, rice and corn, but by throwing the water in which his vegetables are cooked down the waste pipe, he loses another large percentage of it. The animal fed on such refined grains and badly cooked vegetables, dies like the human animal of any disease which happens to take possession of its enfeebled tissues or impoverished blood.

Iron is found nearly chemically pure in a few places, but chemically pure iron is obtained only by artifice. It was described by Berzelious in that state, as very nearly as white as silver, and much softer than ordinary bar-iron. Its uses are too common to receive any attention here, although its appearance in the human body is usually overlooked, when we think of it in horse shoes, nails, hinges, guns and bridges, etc.

Vegetable or animal life is not possible without iron, and yet, notwithstanding the fact that iron is introduced only through the medium of food, the food manufacturer assumes that he has a right to remove it from his product.

MANGANESE.

Manganese has a remarkable affinity for iron, and in some respects bears a close resemblance to iron, with which it is frequently associated. It differs from iron in that while its ores are widely distributed, they are only rarely found in great quantity in any one locality, whereas iron ore exists in abundance in many regions.

It is employed as an oxidizing agent, and its function in the human body is probably very similar to that performed by iron. The physician recognizes its necessity, and frequently endeavors to introduce it into the body as a tonic. He has difficuly in doing this, because his manganese does not appear in the form in which it is found in natural food, and in which it is acceptable to the body.

The food manufacturer does not understand its relationship to normal health, and in consequence is not disturbed over its removal from his product, notwithstanding the fact that it is one of the principal mineral salts always found in the body of a normal animal.

MAGNESIUM.

Loew found that magnesium and phosphorus are intimately associated in the body, and that the metabolism of these two elements in plants is closely connected, magnesium apparently serving as a phosphate carrier in vegetable metabolism just as iron serves as an oxygen carrier in animal metabolism.

Compounds of magnesium are widely distributed in nature, and it is estimated that from 5 to 6 per cent of the solid material held in solution by the water of the ocean is magnesium sulphate, and from 8 to 11 per cent magnesium chloride.

It is a metal of brilliant silver white color, and melts at a red heat. Held in the flame of a candle, it burns with a dazzlingly white light, and for this reason is much employed in the manufacture of flash lights for photography in dark places.

The bones of all animals, and the seeds of various cereals, contain magnesium in the form of a phosphate. Physicians employ magnesium sulphate (epsom salts) in medicine. That magnesium in spite of the important role it plays in the normal functioning of the human body is removed by our artificial processes of refining food does not seem to disturb the food manufacturer unduly.

SULPHUR.

Sulphur occurs in all protein food, associated with nitrogen, but in different proportions. In beans, peas and lentils, the relation is about 50 nitrogen to 1 sulphur; in cheese about 20 nitrogen to 1 sulphur; in egg albumen about 10 nitrogen to 1 sulphur. As protein foods, legumes, meat, cheese, eggs are broken up in the body and oxidized, the sulphur is transformed into sulphuric acid. If this sulphuric acid is not instantly neutralized as rapidly as it is formed, it destroys the tissues. Under an unrefined and natural diet, the body automatically controls this formation of sulphuric acid converting it into inorganic sulphates, which are thrown off for the greater part in the urine. To what extent the kidney cells are broken down by modern artificial foods, robbed of their natural basic elements, or treated with sulphurous acid will never be known. California, Louisiana, and all other states using SO_2 and SO_3 in preparing their dried fruits, sweet wines and molasses do not know the effects of their deadly practices, but our untimely harvest of kidney diseases is on record.

We all know sulphur too well to require its description. Our grandmothers gave it to us in the form of sulphur and molasses. For this reason, the food manufacturer who employs sulphurous acid in bleaching and preserving molasses, dried fruits, glucose and white wines, tells us that we can have no logical objection to it. He does not know that sulphurous acid has none of the properties of sulphur, nor that it is a deadly poison, whereas sulphur even in its pure state cannot be said to be a poison. It is widely distributed in nature in the form of sulphates and sulphides, and is found in all animal and vegetable tissues, but whereas all living bodies, vegetable or animal, require the organized sulphur compounds elaborated by nature they recoil from sulphur dioxide, sulphurous acid and sulphuric acid as actual destroyers of life.

Sulphuric acid, H_2SO_4, is known as oil of vitriol. It is exceedingly corrosive, decomposing all animal and vegetable substances. Sulphurous acid estimated as SO_3, when thrown into water rapidly combines with it to form sulphuric acid. Sulphur dioxide estimated as SO_2, is the colorless, pungent, suffocating gas formed by the combustion of sulphur in air. It is in this state that it is employed in the bleaching of food products, such as all dried apricots, peaches, apples, molasses, etc. It is fatal to life.

Oats or other grains which are treated like dried fruits with sulphur dioxide will not germinate. The so-called "harmless" sulphur processes of the food manufacturer are not in any manner to be confounded with the normal needs of animal or plant life for sulphur in its proper form.

SILICA.

Silica is the commonest of minerals. It is extremely hard, and offers great resistance, even to the oxyhydrogen flame in which it is finally fused to a colorless gas. It is found in the rock crystal amethyst, agate, onyx, jasper, flint, etc.

In the form of quartz, we find it in the sand of the seashore. It occurs in solution in the waters of many mineral springs. It is taken up readily by plant life, and enters the body of the animal through its food, to perform an indispensable function.

Those who for their own purposes tell us that we should not eat silica in the form of the bran of the wheat, on a theory that by so doing we eat "ground glass," do not realize that silica is one of man's mineral needs, and must be appropriated by him in the form in which it appears in his food, in order that his body may be normal. We can't eat the yolk of an egg without eating silica in which it occurs as silicic acid.

SODIUM.

Sodium is another silver white metal with a high lustre. It oxidizes rapidly on exposure to moist air. When heated in ordinary air, it burns rapidly with a bright yellow flame. When thrown into cold water, it oxidizes like potassium, but does not become hot enough to set the liberated hydrogen on fire. At ordinary temperature, it has the consistency of wax, and when melted at less than the boiling point of water, it forms a liquid resembling mercury in appearance. It is next to potassium as the fourth most electropositive metal. In its chemical relations, it is closely allied to potassium, and as a conductor of heat and electricity, it is next to silver, copper and gold.

Two of its compounds are very widely diffused in nature; these are common salt, and sodium carbonate, or ordinary soda. Without sodium in its proper form animal life would not exist.

CHLORINE.

Chlorine is an elementary gaseous substance found in ordinary table salt, and in many forms of vegetable life. It has a yellowish green color, and when inhaled, violently irritates the air passages. It acts as a corrosive agent upon all organic tissues, although in its proper forms, usually as chloride, it is so indispensable to the life of man, that he could not live without it.

FLUORINE.

Fluorine, like chlorine is another gaseous element, which has never been collected in a free state. It forms many compounds with other elements. They are called fluorides, and appear in the teeth and bones of the animal.

As calcium fluoride, it is used in preserving beer, asparagus in glass jars, and also in other foods, although it is one of the most deadly preservatives. Forbidden by law, it is nevertheless used in many places throughout the United States, and in one well known brand of asparagus in glass, its appearance was lately discovered in New York City, and the proper authorities notified, although to date no action has been taken. Brewers use it freely.

Like the other elements entering into the composition of the human body, fluorine appears in its natural state in natural unrefined foods, and in this state is appropriated by the body.

IODINE.

Hunt has found that the resistance of animals to certain poisons differed greatly according to the character of their diet. Bulletin 69, Hygienic Laboratory, U. S. Treasury Department, states: "In extreme cases mice after having been fed upon certain diets may recover from forty times the dose of acetonitrile fatal to mice kept on other diets. It is moreover, possible to alter the resistance of these animals at will, and to overcome the effects of one diet by combining it with another.

The experiments with oats and oatmeal and eggs are of special interest. A diet of oats or oatmeal usually leads to a marked resistance of mice to acetonitrile. The administration of certain iodine compounds with such a diet further increases the resistance. The experiments showed that as far as resistance to acetonitrile is concerned iodine exerts its action through the thyroid gland, and the resistance caused by an oat diet is in part an effect exerted upon the thyroid." All through nature, we find subtle and significant hints that nature knows what she is about in preparing foods that will serve the needs of man in an ideal manner, if man will only co-operate with her, and accept the proposition that her dispensations are not the result of accident, but beautifully ordered, rhythmical processes profound in their operations and benevolent in their results.

Resistance to disease is no new principle in medicine. How do errors of diet, refinement of food, denaturing of the juice of the sugar cane, chemical transformation of starch into glucose, degerminating of corn, wheat, rice, barley, etc., lower that resistance? Yet, unable to answer that question, we go on in our defiance of nature, and refuse to eat the noble foods which she offers and which on animal and man prove their virtue, when here and there some little band of experimenters show the awful results that follow every attempt to refine or process them.

Iodine exists in the water of the ocean, in mineral springs, in marine mollusks, in sea weeds, and in the nitrate deposits of South America.

At ordinary temperature, it is a solid crystaline body, with a bluish black color, and a metallic lustre. It is a non-conductor of electricity, and like oxygen and chlorine, is electro-negative. It combines readily with many other substances, and in these states is known as iodides.

It is an irritant poison, but in its proper form is required by the human body, in which it is chiefly found in the thyroid gland. If one drop of iodine is added to a million drops of water, and a solution of starch dropped into the water, the small quantity of iodine present will give a blue tinge to the mixture.

CARBON.

Carbon is found in nature in two distinctive forms, as the diamond, and as the graphite; the one very hard, the other very soft. It is combustible, and burns to carbonic gas outside the body, or inside the body. Without it, we would have no food. It is the principal constituent of sugar, glucose, starch and fat, although on a diet of pure carbohydrates, man could only live a very short time. Even when fats and proteins are added to pure starch or sugar, the animal fed on such food dies quickly.

No food will support life adequately, unless the minerals described above are present in their proper proportions. Because the food manufacturer does not know this, and because the dietitian has given it so little attention, low resistance is established in tissues nourished on food from which these minerals have been removed by refining processes, and the germs of disease take root and flourish in those tissues.

NITROGEN.

Nitrogen exists in nature as a colorless, odorless, tasteless gas. It is not combustible, nor does it support combustion. It does not enter readily into combination with any other element. It forms about 77 per cent of the weight of the atmosphere, and it is an indispensable constituent in all animal and vegetable tissues.

When introduced into the body in excess quantities, in the form of protein foods, such as meat, cheese and eggs, it induces many serious disorders.

OXYGEN.

Like nitrogen, oxygen is a colorless, odorless, tasteless gas. It combines readily with most of the elements, except fluorine. It is so energetic in its act of combining with these substances that in many instances it evolves light and heat, and bursts into flame. In other instances combination takes place so slowly, that while the result is the same, the heat evolved at one time is not sufficient to produce a flame, or even to be noticed.

The tarnishing or rusting of metals, and the decay of animal or vegetable substances, are instances of this slow combustion. Without free oxygen there would be no animal or vegetable life. The heat of the body, and the energy of the muscles are the results of slow combustion produced in all parts of the body, by oxygen carried into the system from the lungs, by the iron in the blood.

HYDROGEN.

Like oxygen and nitrogen, hydrogen is a colorless, tasteless, odorless gas. It is the lightest substance known in nature. It burns in air with a very pale blue flame and intense heat, the only product of its combustion being pure water. It is usually found only in combination with other substances, although it occurs free in the gases of volcanoes, and of some oil wells. No animal or vegetable structure can exist without it. It is a component of all acids. When driven out of acids by bases, the acids are transformed into salts, and it is thus that we get the mineral salts of the earth into our bodies. Its function in the processes of life are as important as that of any of the substances we have considered, but no more so.

It is the combination of all these substances in proper and orderly proportion that sustains life. We can thus see why those who prepare our food, have no right to artificially treat that food; to denature, debase, degerminate, demineralize, refine or chemically change the character of that food.

When this naked truth is learned by our legislators, we will have a new and wholesome food situation in the United States, and a newer, wholesomer, sturdier and better race of men.

STARVING THE POOR.

The yolk of the hen's egg, analyzed by Gautier, provides in the food of the child:

Water ....47.19—51.49
Solids ....48.51—42.81
    Fats ....21.30—22.84
    Vitellin ....15.63—15.76
    Lecithins .... 8.43—10.72
    Cholesterin .... 0.44— 1.75
    Mineral Salts .... 3.33— 0.36

Poleck and Weber, analyzing 100 parts yolk ash, give the following as the yolk's contribution through its mineral salts to the diet of the child:

Sodium (Na_2O) .... 5.12— 6.57

Potassium (K₂O) .... 8.05— 8.93
Calcium (CaO) ....12.21—13.28
Magnesium (MgO) .... 2.07— 2.11
Iron (Fe₂O₃) .... 1.19— 1.45
Phosphoric acid, free (P₂O₅) . 5.72— 5.72
Phosphoric acid, combined ..63.81—66.70
Silicic acid (SiO₂).......... 0.55— 1.40
Chlorine .... traces

Cold storage provides a noble means of carrying this precious food-material from abundant periods to lean months, at a legitimate profit to the egg industry, thus giving to the child a food without which under our modern standards of debased supplies, there is no hope that the necessary body-building materials may be found in adequate quantity.

In spite of the warm weather that prevailed during October and November, 1912, during which time millions of eggs were shipped from all parts of the country to the already well supplied storage houses of New York and Philadelphia, an artificial famine was created by the holders of supplies.

At this writing (November 28, 1912) "fresh" eggs are selling in New York at 60 to 65 cents a dozen and storage eggs are selling at 40 cents and 45 cents a dozen. They cost less than 20 cents a dozen when they went into storage. The dealers predict $1.00 eggs during January. This condition, under a knowledge of the meaning of the egg to child-life, is so monstrous, inhuman, unnatural and intolerable that those who speculate in the indispensable staples of life, controlling as they do the very health and happiness of the weak and defenseless, should be treated as any other menace of society is treated. They are murderers in fact, though by judge and jury, under our present dispensation, they will never be held so.

It is the duty of our medical associations to go on record concerning issues so indissolubly bound with the problems of life and death.

This chapter was the subject of the author's address before the Eastern Medical Association at Hotel Astor, New York, Dec. 3, 1912.

SALTS OF TIN.

Corn, peas, tomatoes, hominy, kraut, and sweet potatoes, cause the least re-action upon the tin in which they are packed and are the safest of the canned vegetables.

Plums, peaches, apricots, white cherries, lima beans, apples, pork and beans in tomato sauce, tomato soup, and cider act on the tin, and produce tin salts, which the trade believes not to be in excess, and any interference with which is resented.

Apparently enamel-lined tins prevent the formation of tin salts. The public should be in possession of the plain facts, and the physician should know the physiological action of tin, not only on the body, but on the other chemical agents which his prescription calls for.

Apple butter, blackberries, blueberries, pumpkin, black raspberries, red raspberries, red cherries, beets, squash, string beans, wax beans and strawberries become actually dangerous, unless packed in glass or tins that are enamel-lined. The canners know this. In fact this information reaches the public through the canner's own laboratories, but not with their knowledge or approval. The Bureau of Chemistry has not instructed the public in this regard. Its apparent duty is not to interfere with "business."

Spinach, unless packed solid, is not safe in any style tin. Rhubarb should not be packed in tin of any kind.

ANALYSIS OF A GRAIN OF WHEAT.

Following is an analysis which varies slightly, depending on character of wheat:

Water 12%
Protein 13%
Fat 2%
Carbohydrates . } 71%
(Sugar, starch)

Mineral salts. . . . 2%
———
100%

Mineral Analysis:
Potassium . . . 30.50
K_2O
Sodium 2.20
Na_2O
Calcium 3.20
CaO
Magnesium . . 12.00
MgO
Iron 1.50
Fe_2O_3
Phosphorus . . 46.00
P_2O_5
Sulphur 50
SO_3
Silicon 2.00
SiO_2
Chlorine 33
Cl
Fluorine . . . . . traces
Iodine . . . . . . traces
Manganese . . traces

This mineral content of the whole wheat is 2%.

The mineral content of white flour is reduced to one-half of one per cent.

Glucose makers put all the mineral content of the corn back into their cattle feed, admitting that if they do not the cattle will die.

The parts of the wheat berry marked a, skin
and testa; b, membrane; c, embryo; e, cereal or
aleurone layer; f, scutulum, contain three-fourths of
the mineral salts of the grain. These parts when
removed, are known as bran, shorts, coarse middlings, fine middlings, and tailings.

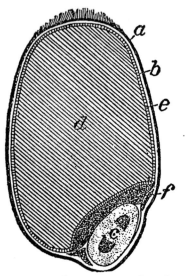

Fig. 1 —Diagrammatic section of
grain of wheat: a, skin and testa;
b, membrane; c, embryo; d, flour
cells; e, cereal or aleuronc layer,
f, scutulum.

This year's wheat crop, 695,443,000 bushels, will
reach the human family in a minerally robbed condition, because the fine white flour has thrown all
these elements out in the milling process. Hardly a
bushel of that wheat will be consumed by man, as
mother nature prepared it.

The illustration of the wheat berry, of which
section d represents the fine white flour, 72% pure

starch, will. also serve to give you an understanding of the formation of barley, rice, oats, and corn, all of which are robbed, just as wheat is robbed, with the exception of the small proportion of cut oats, or whole oat meal, which reaches the consumer in a natural state.

The corn crop of 1912 is estimated at 3,125,713,-000 bushels. Few bushels of that grain will reach

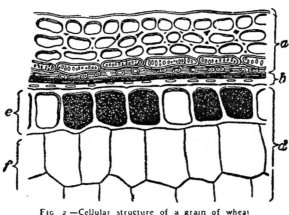

Fig 2 —Cellular structure of a grain of wheat
(After Winton and Moeller)

the needs of man as mother nature furnishes it for those needs.

It is de-germinated and de-mineralized just as wheat is debased. The tragedy of our ignorant and wanton destruction of the corn crop of America can only be appreciated by those who understand the full significance of our 15 million physically defective school children.

The author is indebted to the following, many of them without their knowledge, for physiological data, enthusiasm for the cause or for personal sympathy and encouragement.

Dr. G. C. Simpson, Liverpool School of Tropical Medicine, University of Liverpool.

Professor Benjamin Moore, Professor of Bio-Chemistry, University of Liverpool.

Dr. Frederick Gowland Hopkins, F. R. S., Reader in Chemical Physiology at the University of Cambridge.

Dr. Franklin Armstrong, British Association.

James R. Mitchell, M. D., Lecturer in Chemistry, Fort Worth University Medical College.

Dr. E. S. Edie
Dr. F. M. Anderson
Dr. Leonard Hill
Dr. Fletcher, Burma
Dr. W. B. Carpenter
Dr. Pavy, F. R. S.
Dr. Beddoe, F. R. S.
Professor Rae Lankester, F. R. S.
Sir B. W. W. Richardson, F. R. S.
Dr. Frankland Armstrong
Sir James Crichton Browne, M. D., LL. D.
Dr. Marcet, F. R. S.
Sir Lauder Brunton
Dr. G. A. Heron
Mr. A. P. Gould
Dr. J. S. Sykes
Dr. W. R. Smith
Dr. David Walsh
Mr. A. M. Robeson
Dr. Dyce Brown

Miss May Yates
Sir W. B. Richmond
Dr. R. Bevan
Sir Wm. Collins, M. D.
Dr. Stanford Read
Sir Robert Matheson
Dr. Nathan Raw
Dr. Alice Kerr
Dr. Robert Kaye
Dr. Lena Fox, Bermondsey Medical Mission
Dr. Garrow Grant
Dr. V. G. Heiser, Manila
Dr. Highet, Siam
Dr. Aaron, Philippine Medical School
Dr. De Haan, Java
Dr. Fraser, Singapore
Frederick C. Johnson
J. W. Kjelgaard
E. F. Wright
Harvey W. Wiley
Lewis B. Allyn
Otto Carque
Floyd W. Robison

CPSIA information can be obtained at www.ICGtesting.com
Printed in the USA
LVOW06s1801030714

392893LV00004B/944/P

9 781429 012034